The Elements
of
C# *Style*

Kenneth Baldwin
CenterSpace Software

Andrew Gray
Evolution Software
Design

Trevor Misfeldt
CenterSpace Software

CAMBRIDGE
UNIVERSITY PRESS

CAMBRIDGE UNIVERSITY PRESS
Cambridge, New York, Melbourne, Madrid, Cape Town, Singapore, São Paulo

Cambridge University Press
32 Avenue of the Americas, New York, NY 10013-2473, USA

www.cambridge.org
Information on this title: www.cambridge.org/

© Cambridge University Press 2006

This publication is in copyright. Subject to statutory exception
and to the provisions of relevant collective licensing agreements,
no reproduction of any part may take place without
the written permission of Cambridge University Press.

First published 2006

Printed in the United States of America

A catalog record for this publication is available from the British Library.

Library of Congress Cataloging in Publication Data

Baldwin, Kenneth.
The Elements of C# style / Kenneth Baldwin, Andrew Gray, Trevor
Misfeldt.
  p. cm.
Includes bibliographical references and index.
ISBN-13: 978-0-521-67159-0 (paperback)
ISBN-10: 0-521-67159-0 (paperback)
1. C# (Computer program language)   I. Gray, Andrew, 1971–
II. Misfeldt, Trevor, 1969–   III. Title
QA76.73.C154B36   2006
005.13'3 – dc22   2006008307

ISBN-13   978-0-521-67159-0 paperback
ISBN-10   0-521-67159-0 paperback

Cambridge University Press has no responsibility for
the persistence or accuracy of URLs for external or
third-party Internet Web sites referred to in this publication
and does not guarantee that any content on such
Web sites is, or will remain, accurate or appropriate.

Contents

Preface

As commercial developers of software components, we always strive to have good, consistent style throughout our code. Since source code is usually included in our final products, our users often study our code to learn not just how the components work, but also how to write good software.

This fact ultimately led to the creation of *The Elements of Java Style*[1] and *The Elements of C++ Style*.[2] The positive reception of those books, coupled with recurring questions about C# and .NET style issues, resulted in this edition for C#.

If you've read the earlier books in this series (or even if you haven't), much of the advice in this book will probably be familiar. This is deliberate, as many of the programming principles described are timeless and valid across programming languages. However, the content has been reworked and expanded here to address the unique characteristics of the C# language.

Audience

We wrote this book for anyone writing C# code, but especially for programmers who are writing C# as part of a team. For a team to be effective, everyone must be able to read and

---

[1] Vermeulen, Al, et al. *The Elements of Java Style*. (Cambridge, UK: Cambridge University Press, 2000).
[2] Misfeldt, Trevor, Greg Bumgardner, and Andrew Gray. *The Elements of C++ Style*. (Cambridge, UK: Cambridge University Press, 2004).

understand everyone else's code. Having consistent style conventions is a good first step!

This book is not intended to teach you C#, but rather it focuses on how C# code can be written in order to maximize its effectiveness. We therefore assume you are already familiar with C# and object-oriented programming.

Introduction

> style: 1b. the shadow-producing pin of a sundial.
> 2c. the custom or plan followed in spelling,
> capitalization, punctuation, and typographic
> arrangement and display.
> —*Webster's New Collegiate Dictionary*

The syntax of a programming language tells you what code it is possible to write—what machines will understand. Style tells you what you ought to write—what humans reading the code will understand. Code written with a consistent, simple style is maintainable, robust, and contains fewer bugs. Code written with no regard to style contains more bugs, and may simply be thrown away and rewritten rather than maintained.

Attending to style is particularly important when developing as a team. Consistent style facilitates communication, because it enables team members to read and understand each other's work more easily. In our experience, the value of consistent programming style grows exponentially with the number of people working with the code.

Our favorite style guides are classics: Strunk and White's *The Elements of Style*[3] and Kernighan and Plauger's *The Elements of Programming Style*.[4] These small books work because they

---

[3] Strunk, William Jr., and E. B. White. *The Elements of Style, Fourth Edition*. (Allyn & Bacon, 2000).
[4] Kernighan, Brian and P. J. Plauger. *The Elements of Programming Style*. (New York: McGraw-Hill, 1988).

are simple: a list of rules, each containing a brief explanation and examples of correct, and sometimes incorrect, use. We followed the same pattern in this book. This simple treatment—a series of rules—enabled us to keep this book short and easy to understand.

Some of the advice that you read here may seem obvious to you, particularly if you've been writing code for a long time. Others may disagree with some of our specific suggestions about formatting or indentation. The most important thing is consistency. What we've tried to do here is distill many decades of development experience into an easily accessible set of heuristics that encourage consistent coding practice (and hopefully help you avoid some coding traps along the way). The idea is to provide a clear standard to follow so programmers can spend their time on solving the problems of their customers instead of worrying about things like naming conventions and formatting.

The guidelines in this book complement the official .NET design guidelines in the ECMA C# specification[5] and Krzysztof Cwalina and Brad Abrams' excellent *Framework Design Guidelines*.[6] This book extends those guidelines to internal implementation and coding style.

Disclaimer

We have dramatically simplified the code samples used in this book to highlight the concepts related to a particular rule. In many cases, these code fragments do not conform to

---

[5] ECMA International, Standard ECMA-334: "C# Language Specification." 3rd Edition, June 2005. http://www.ecma-international.org/publications/standards/Ecma-334.htm.

[6] Cwalina, Krzysztof and Brad Abrams. *Framework Design Guidelines: Conventions, Idioms, and Patterns for Reusable .NET Libraries.* Addison-Wesley, 2005. ISBN 0321246756.

conventions described elsewhere in this book—they lack real documentation and fail to meet certain minimum declarative requirements. Do not treat these fragments as definitive examples of real code!

Acknowledgments

Books like these are necessarily a team effort. Major contributions came from the original authors of *The Elements of Java Style*: Al Vermeulen, Scott Ambler, Greg Bumgardner, Eldon Metz, Trevor Misfeldt, Jim Shur, and Patrick Thompson, and the original authors of *The Elements of C++ Style*: Trevor Misfeldt, Greg Bumgardner, and Andrew Gray. Both of those books have some roots in "C++ Design, Implementation, and Style Guide," written by Tom Keffer, the "Rogue Wave Java Style Guide," and the "Ambysoft Inc. Coding Standards for Java," documents to which Jeremy Smith, Tom Keffer, Wayne Gramlich, Pete Handsman, and Cris Perdue all contributed.

Thanks also to the reviewers who provided valuable feedback on drafts of this book, particularly Brad Abrams, Krzysztof Cwalina, and Mark Vulfson of Microsoft Corporation; Mike Gunderloy of Larkware; and Michael Gerfen of Evolution Software Design.

This book would certainly never have happened without the help and encouragement of the folks at Cambridge University Press, particularly Jessica Farris and Lauren Cowles, who kept us on track throughout the writing and publication process.

1.

General Principles

While it is important to write software that performs well, many other issues should concern the professional developer. *Good* software gets the job done. But *great* software, written with a consistent style, is predictable, robust, maintainable, supportable, and extensible.

1. Adhere to the Style of the Original

When modifying existing software, your changes should follow the style of the original code.[7] Do not introduce a new coding style in a modification, and do not attempt to rewrite the old software just to make it match the new style. The use of different styles within a single source file produces code that is more difficult to read and comprehend. Rewriting old code simply to change its style may result in the introduction of costly yet avoidable defects.

2. Adhere to the Principle of Least Astonishment

The *Principle of Least Astonishment* suggests you should avoid doing things that would surprise other software developers. This implies that the means of interaction and the behavior exhibited by your software must be predictable and

---

[7] Jim Karabatsos. "When does this document apply?" In "Visual Basic Programming Standards." (GUI Computing Ltd., 22 March 1996).

consistent,[8] and, if not, the documentation must clearly identify and justify any unusual patterns of use or behavior.

To minimize the chances that anyone would encounter something surprising in your software, you should emphasize the following characteristics in the design, implementation, packaging, and documentation of your software:

Simplicity	Meet the expectations of your users with simple classes and simple methods.
Clarity	Ensure that each class, interface, method, variable, and object has a clear purpose. Explain where, when, why, and how to use each.
Completeness	Provide the minimum functionality that any reasonable user would expect to find and use. Create complete documentation; document all features and functionality.
Consistency	Similar entities should look and behave the same; dissimilar entities should look and behave differently. Create and apply consistent standards whenever possible.
Robustness	Provide predictable, documented behavior in response to errors and exceptions. Do not hide errors and do not force clients to detect errors.

3. Do It Right the First Time

Apply these rules to any code you write, not just code destined for production. More often than not, some piece of prototype

---

[8] George Brackett. "Class 6: Designing for Communication: Layout, Structure, Navigation for Nets and Webs." In "Course T525: Designing Educational Experiences for Networks and Webs." (Harvard Graduate School of Education, 26 August 1999).

or experimental code will make its way into a finished product, so you should anticipate this eventuality. Even if your code never makes it into production, someone else may still have to read it. Anyone who must look at your code will appreciate your professionalism and foresight at having consistently applied these rules from the start.

4. Document Any Deviations

No standard is perfect and no standard is universally applicable. Sometimes you will find yourself in a situation where you need to deviate from an established standard. Regardless, strive for clarity and consistency.

Before you decide to ignore a rule, you should first make sure you understand why the rule exists and what the consequences are if it is not applied. If you decide you must violate a rule, then document why you have done so.

This is the *prime directive*.

5. Consider Using a Code-Checking Tool to Enforce Coding Standards

A source code analysis tool enables you to check your code for compliance with coding standards and best practices. For example, FxCop[9] is a popular .NET code analysis tool that uses reflection, MSIL parsing, and callgraph analysis to check for conformance to the .NET Framework design guidelines. FxCop is extensible, and can thus incorporate the particular coding standards used by your own organization.

---

[9] http://www.gotdotnet.com/team/fxcop/.

2.

Formatting

2.1 White Space

6. Include White Space

White space is the area on a page devoid of visible characters. Code with too little white space is difficult to read and understand, so use plenty of white space to delineate methods, comments, code blocks, and expressions clearly.

Use a single space to separate the keywords, parentheses, and curly braces in control flow statements:

```
for·(...)
{
  //...
}

while·(...)
{
  //...
}

do
{
  //...
}·while·(...);

switch·(...)
{
  //...
}
```

```
if · (...)
{
  //...
}
else · if · (...)
{
  //...
}
else
{
  //...
}

try
{
  //...
}
catch · (Exception)
{
  //...
}
finally
{
  //...
}
```

Use a single space on either side of binary operators, except for the "." operator:

```
double length = Math.Sqrt(x * x + y * y);
double xNorm = (length > 0.0) ? (x / length) : x;
double currentTemperature =
    engineBlock.Temperature;
```

Use a single space after commas and semicolons:

```
Vector normalizedVector =
    NormalizeVector(x, y, z);

for (int i = 0; i < 100; i++)
{
  //...
}
```

Use a single space between the parentheses for the parameter list in a method declaration:

```
Vector NormalizeVector(double x, double y,
                       double z)
{
  //...
}
```

Use blank lines to separate each logical section of a method body:

```
public void HandleMessage(Message message)
{
  string content = message.ReadContent();
  switch (message.ErrorLevel)
  {
    case ErrorLevel.Warning:
      //... do some stuff here ...
      break;
    case ErrorLevel.Severe:
      //... do some stuff here ...
      break;
    default:
      //... do some stuff here ...
      break;
  }
}
```

Use blank lines to separate each method definition in a class:

```csharp
public void SendEmail()
{
  //...
}

public void SendFax()
{
  //...
}
```

7. Use Indented Block Statements

One way to improve code readability is to group individual statements into block statements and uniformly indent the content of each block to set off its contents from the surrounding code.

If you generate code using an integrated development environment (such as Visual Studio), make sure that everyone on your team uses consistent indentation options. If you are generating the code by hand, use two spaces to ensure readability without taking up too much space (see Rule #9):

```csharp
void PesterCustomer(Customer customer)
{
  customer.SendLetter();
  if (customer.HasEmailAddress())
  {
    customer.SendEmail();
    if (customer.IsForgetful())
    {
      customer.ScheduleReminderEmail();
    }
  }
  if (customer.HasFaxNumber())
  {
```

```
    customer.SendFax();
  }
}
```

If you are managing a development team, do not leave it up to individual developers to choose their own indentation amount and style. Establish a standard indentation policy for the organization and ensure that everyone complies with this standard.

8. *Indent Statements after a Label*

In addition to indenting the contents of block statements, you should also indent the statements that follow a label to make the label easier to notice:

```
void DoSomethingUseful(int arg)
{
  loop:
    for (int index = 0; index <= arg; index++)
    {
      switch (index)
      {
        case 0:
          //...
          break; // exit the switch statement
        default:
          //...
          break; // exit the switch statement
    }
  }
}
```

9. *Do Not Use "Hard" Tabs*

Many developers use tab characters to indent and align their source code without realizing that the interpretation of tab characters varies across environments. Code that appears to possess the correct formatting when viewed in the original editing environment can appear unformatted and virtually unreadable when viewed by another developer or transported to an environment that interprets tabs differently.

To avoid this problem, always use spaces instead of tabs to indent and align source code. You may do this simply by using the space bar instead of the tab key or by configuring your editor to replace tabs with spaces. Some editors also provide a "smart" indentation capability. You should disable this feature if it uses tab characters.

10. *Break Long Statements into Multiple Lines*

While a modern window-based editor can easily handle long source code lines by scrolling horizontally, it is more productive and less error-prone for developers to read code on one screen without having to scroll. In addition, a printer must truncate, wrap, or print on separate sheets any lines that exceed its maximum printable line width. To ensure your source code is still readable when printed, you should limit your source code line lengths to the maximum width your printing environment supports, typically 80 to 132 characters.

First, do not place multiple statement expressions on a single line if the result is a line that exceeds your maximum allowable line length. If two statement expressions are placed on one line,

```
double x = random.NextDouble(); double y =
random.NextDouble(); // Too Long!
```

then introduce a new line to place them on separate lines:

```
double x = random.NextDouble();
double y = random.NextDouble();
```

Second, if a line is too long because it contains a complex expression,

```
double distance = Math.Sqrt(Math.Pow((x1 - x2), 2.0)
+ Math.Pow((y1 - y2), 2.0) + Math.Pow(z1 - z2), 2.0));
// Too Long!
```

then subdivide the expression into several smaller subexpressions for clarity. Use a separate line to store the result produced by an evaluation of each subexpression into a temporary variable:

```
double dx = Math.Pow((x1 - x2), 2.0);
double dy = Math.Pow((y1 - y2), 2.0);
double dz = Math.Pow((z1 - z2), 2.0);
double distance = Math.Sqrt(dx + dy + dz);
```

Last, if a long line cannot be shortened under the preceding guidelines, then break, wrap, and indent that line using the following rules.

Step one:

If the top-level expression on the line contains one or more commas,

```
double value = Foo(Math.Pow(x, 2.0),
Math.Pow(y, 2.0), Math.Pow(z, 2.0));
// Too Long!
```

then introduce a line break after each comma. Align each expression following a comma with the first character of the expression preceding the comma:

```
double value = Foo(Math.Pow(x, 2.0),
                   Math.Pow(y, 2.0),
                   Math.Pow(z, 2.0));
```

Step two:

If the top-level expression on the line contains no commas:

```
return person1.Name == person2.Name &&
person1.Address == person2.Address &&
person1.Phone == person2.Phone; // Too Long!
```

then introduce a line break just before the operator with the lowest precedence; or, if more than one operator of equally low precedence exists between each such operator, align them like this:

```
return person1.Name == person2.Name &&
       person1.Address == person2.Address &&
       person1.Phone == person2.Phone;
```

Step three:

Reapply steps one and two, as required, until each line created from the original statement expression is less than the maximum allowable length.

2.2 Braces

11. Choose One Style for Brace Placement

You have two choices for placing the opening brace of a block statement: you may place the brace at the end of the line that controls entry into the block, or you may place it on the next line and align it with the first character of the first line. You should always place the closing brace on a line of its own and align it with the first character of the line containing the opening brace:

```
void SameLine() {
}

void NextLine()
{
}
```

While many programmers use one or both of these styles, your organization should choose one style and apply it consistently.

In this book, we use the second style of brace placement. The following examples illustrate how this rule applies to each of the various C# definition and control constructs.

Class definitions:

```
namespace MyOrganization
{
  public class Outer
  {
    public Outer()
    {
      //...
    }

    public class Inner
    {
      public Inner()
      {
        //...
      }
    }
  }
}
```

Method declarations:

```
public void Display()
{
  //...
}
```

For-loop statements:

```
for (int i = 0; i <= j; i++)
{
  //...
}
```

If and else statements:

```
if (j < 0)
{
  //...
}
else if (j > 0)
{
  //...
}
else
{
  //...
}
```

Try, catch blocks:

```
try
{
  //...
}
catch (...)
{
  //...
}
finally
{
  //...
}
```

Switch statements:

```
switch (value)
{
  case 0:
    //...
```

```
    break;
  default:
    //...
    break;
}
```

While statements:

```
while (++k <= j)
{
  //...
}
```

Do-while statements:

```
do
{
  //...
} while (++k <= j);
```

12. *Always Use Block Statements in Control Flow Constructs*

A compound or block statement provides a mechanism for treating any number of statements as a single compound statement. The various control flow statements, if..else, for, while, and do..while, provide the means for conditionally executing a single statement or a block.

You must use blocks if you wish to conditionally execute multiple statements as part of a control flow statement. You may also need to use blocks when nesting if..else statements to avoid a potential ambiguity often referred to as the "dangling else problem."

```
if (x >= 0)
  if (x > 0) PositiveX();
else // Oops! Matches most recent if!
```

```
NegativeX();
```

While this is more verbose, the logic flow is clear and maintainable:

```
if (x >= 0)
{
  if (x > 0)
  {
    PositiveX();
  }
  else
  {
    // Do nothing...
  }
}
else
{
  NegativeX(); // This is what we intended!
}
```

When you use blocks, you make it easier to add additional statements to an existing control flow construct:

```
for (int i = n; i >= 0; i--)
  for (int j = n; j >= 0; j--)
    Foo(i, j);
    Goo(i, j); // Why are i and j out of scope?
for (int i = n; i >= 0; i--)
{
  for (int j = n; j >= 0; j--)
  {
    Foo(i, j);
    Goo(i, j); // This is what we intended!
  }
}
```

2.3 Class Organization

13. *Group Using Directives at the Top of a Source File*

When a source file makes use of `using` directives, group them together at the top of the file. List system-defined namespaces in alphabetical order, followed by a blank line; then third party namespaces in alphabetical order, followed by a blank line; then user-defined namespaces in alphabetical order.

```
using System;
using System.IO;
using System.Xml;

using CenterSpace.NMath.Core;
using CenterSpace.NMath.Stats;

using MyOrganization.BusinessUtilities;
```

14. *Organize Source Code into Regions*

Organize each source file into meaningful regions, using the `#region...#endregion` construct. With many development environments (such as Microsoft Visual Studio), users can collapse regions to facilitate viewing of large source files.

Establish a fixed list and ordering of regions for your development organization. For example, you might use something like the following (mirroring the organization of MSDN-style documentation pages):

- Public constructors
- Public properties
- Public methods
- Event handlers
- Private fields
- Private methods

15. Order Class Elements by Access

Within a source file, order declarations by their access modifiers:

- public
- protected
- internal
- private

Within an access modifier grouping, list declarations alphabetically.

16. Declare Each Variable and Attribute Separately

Declare each variable on a separate line. That is, don't do this:

```
int x = 12, y = 18;
```

or this:

```
int x = 12; int y = 18;
```

Instead use separate lines for each declaration:

```
int x = 12;
int y = 18;
```

See also Rule #10.

Place each attribute on a separate line for clarity. That is, don't do this:

```
[Serializable(), Conditional("DEBUG")]
public class SerializableDebugObject
{
  //...
}
```

Instead do this:

```
[Serializable()]
[Conditional("DEBUG")]
public class SerializableDebugObject
{
  //...
}
```

3.

Naming

Consistent use of naming conventions can provide valuable visual cues to those reading the code you write. This chapter recommends conventions that can make your code more readable.

3.1 General

17. *Use Meaningful Names*

Use names that are, and will remain, meaningful to those who will eventually read your code. Use meaningful words to create names. Agree on a consistent language which can be understood by future users. Avoid using a single character or generic names that do little to define the purpose of the entities they name.

The purpose for the variable a and the constant 65 in the following code is unclear:

```
if (a < 65)
{
  // What property does 'a' describe?
  // What is being calculated here?
  y = 65 - a;
}
else
{
  y = 0;
}
```

The code is much easier to understand when meaningful names are used:

```
if (age < RetirementAge)
{
  yearsToRetirement = RetirementAge - age;
}
else
{
  yearsToRetirement = 0;
}
```

The only exception to this rule concerns temporary variables whose context provides sufficient information to determine their purpose, such as a variable used as a counter or index within a loop (see Rule #47):

```
for (int i = 0; i < numberOfStudents; ++i)
{
  EnrollStudent(i);
}
```

18. Name According to Meaning Not Type

Type information can generally be inferred from usage and context. Keep your names useful by attaching meaning to them. For example, use Customer instead of CustomerClass.

An exception to the rule exists for GUI controls. It can sometimes be very useful to be able to differentiate the type of GUI element by name. For example, it would be useful to distinguish customerNameLabel (a label on a form) from customerNameTextbox (a textbox on a form).[10]

---

[10] http://pluralsight.com/blogs/fritz/archive/2004/12/29/4178.aspx.

19. Use Familiar Names

Use words that exist in the terminology of the target domain. If your users refer to "customers," then use the name `Customer` for the class, not `Client`. Many developers make the mistake of creating new or generic terms for concepts when satisfactory terms already exist in the target industry or domain.

20. Do Not Use Case to Differentiate Names

Compilers can distinguish between names that differ only in case, but a human reader may fail to notice the difference. This is equivalent to name hiding.

For example, do not name a class `XmlStream` if a class named `XMLStream` already exists. If both names appear in the same scope, each effectively hides the other when considered from the perspective of a person trying to read and understand the code.

21. Avoid Excessively Long Names

The name given an object must adequately describe its purpose. If a class, interface, variable, or method has an overly long name, then that entity is probably trying to accomplish too much.

Instead of simply giving the entity a new name that conveys less meaning, first reconsider its design or purpose. A refactoring of the entity may produce new classes, interfaces, methods, or variables that are more focused and can be given more meaningful yet simpler names.

22. Join the Vowel Generation—Use Complete Words

Do not attempt to shorten names by removing vowels. This practice reduces the readability of your code and introduces ambiguity if more than one meaningful name reduces to the same consonants.

Replace:

```
public class Msg
{
  public Msg AppndSig(string sig)
  {
    . . .
  }
}
```

With:

```
public class Message
{
  public Message AppendSignature(string signature)
  {
    . . .
  }
}
```

The casual reader can understand the names in the latter implementation.

If you find yourself removing vowels simply to shorten a long name, then you need to question whether the original name is appropriate (see Rule #21).

3.2 Abbreviations

23. *Avoid Abbreviations Unless the Full Name Is Excessive*

Resist confusing people with unnecessary abbreviations. Substituting Grph for Graphical is unnecessary, but GuiListener is preferable to GraphicalUserInterfaceListener. If you must use an abbreviation, use one that is widely used and accepted.

24. *Format Abbreviations Like Regular Words*

If an abbreviation appears as the first word in a type or constant, only capitalize the first letter of the abbreviation.

Use this style to eliminate confusion in names where uppercase letters act as word separators. This is especially important if one abbreviation immediately follows another:

```
XMLString > XmlString
LoadXMLDocument() > LoadXmlDocument()
```

This rule does not apply to abbreviations that appear within the name of a conditional compilation symbol because these names only contain capital letters (see Rule #25):

```
[conditional(GUI)]
```

The rule does not apply to abbreviations that appear at the beginning of a variable or parameter name because these names should always start with a lowercase letter:

```
Document xmlDocument;
```

3.3 Preprocessor Symbols

25. *Use Uppercase and Underscores for Preprocessor Symbols*

The capitalization of preprocessor names distinguishes them from symbols defined using C# grammar:

```
#define EVAL_VERSION
```

26. *Add a Unique Prefix to Preprocessor Names*

Add a prefix to preprocessor names to create names that will not conflict with those defined in user or third-party software. We recommend that you add an abbreviation that identifies your organization and, optionally, an abbreviation that identifies your product: for example, ACME_DB_USER.

3.4 Types and Constants

27. Use Pascal Case for Namespaces, Classes, Structures, Properties, Enumerations, Constants, and Functions

Capitalize the first letter of each word to provide a visual cue for separating the individual words within a name. The leading capital letter provides a mechanism for differentiating them from parameters or variables (see Rule #43):

```
public enum BackgroundColor
{
  None = 0,
  Red = 1,
  Green = 2,
  Blue = 3
};

const int FixedWidth = 10;

class BankAccount
{
  //...
}

public double CalculatePercentile(double percent)
{
  //...
}
```

28. Use Nouns to Name Compound Types

Classes, structs, or properties that define objects, or things, should be identified by nouns:

```
public class Customer
{
  public string Name
  {
    get
    {
      return name_;
    }
  }
  //...
}
```

29. Pluralize the Names of Collections

Collections of objects should have a name that corresponds to the plural form of the object type contained in the collection. This enables a reader of your code to distinguish between variables representing multiple values from those representing single values:

```
List<Shape> shapes = ...
Shape shape = shapes[index];
```

30. Suffix Abstract Base Types with "Base"

Clearly defined base classes are easier to manage.

```
public abstract class AccountBase
public class PersonalAccount : AccountBase
public class BusinessAccount : AccountBase
```

31. Append the Pattern Name to Classes Implementing a Design Pattern

For example, a class named MessageFactory implies certain behaviors to developers who are familiar with design patterns.

32. Use a Single Capital Letter for Generic Parameters

```
public static List <T> Uniquify(List <T>)
{
  //...
}
```

3.5 Enumerations

33. Use Singular Names for Enumerations

Enumerated types are generally used for lists of mutually exclusive elements, and should be singular:

```
public enum SortOrder
```

34. Use Plural Names for Bitfields

Bit fields are generally used for lists of elements that can occur in combination and should be plural:

```
[Flags]
public enum PrintSettings
{
  Draft = 0,
  Duplex = 1,
  Color = 2
};
```

See also Rule #136.

3.6 Interfaces

35. Prefix Interface Names with a Capital Letter "I"

It is convenient to know whether a class is inheriting from a parent class or implementing an interface.

```
public class Worker : IWorkable
```

36. *Use Nouns or Adjectives When Naming Interfaces*

An interface provides a declaration of the services provided by an object, or it provides a description of the capabilities of an object.

Use nouns to name interfaces that act as service declarations:

```
public interface IMessageListener
{
  public void MessageReceived(Message message);
}
```

Use adjectives to name interfaces that act as descriptions of capabilities. Most interfaces that describe capabilities use an adjective created by tacking an -able or -ible suffix onto the end of a verb:

```
public interface IReversible
{
  public ICollection Reverse();
}
```

3.7 Properties

37. *Name Properties after the Item They Get or Set*

For example, a property that gets an expiration date:

```
public Date ExpirationDate
{
  get
  {
    return expirationDate_;
  }
}
```

38. *Avoid Redundant Property Names*

Prefer

```
public ICollection Customers
```

to

```
public ICollection CustomerCollection
```

39. *Name Boolean Properties to Indicate Their Boolean Nature*

If a property returns a boolean, prefix the name with "is", "has", or "are".

```
public bool IsGood
public bool HasCompleted
```

3.8 Methods

40. *Use Pascal Case for Method Names*

Use uppercase for the first word and capitalize each subsequent word that appears in a function name to provide a visual cue for separating the individual words within each name.

```
public class DataManipulator
{
  public void ComputeStatistics(DoubleMatrix m);
}
```

41. *Use Verbs to Name Methods*

Methods commonly define *actions*, which are described by verbs:

```
public class Account
{
  public void Withdraw(double amount)
```

```
  {
    balance_ -= amount;
  }
  public void Deposit(double amount)
  {
    Withdraw(-amount);
  }
}
```

42. Avoid Redundant Method Names

In a Book class, prefer this:

```
public void Open()
```

to:

```
public void OpenBook()
```

3.9 Variables and Parameters

43. Use Camel Case for Variable and Method Parameter Names

Use lowercase for the first word and capitalize each subsequent word that appears in a variable name to provide a visual cue for separating the individual words within each name.

```
public class Customer
{
  public string firstName_;
  public string lastName_;

  public string ToString()
  {
    return lastName_ + ", " + firstName_;
  }
}
```

The leading lowercase letter provides a mechanism for differentiating between variables and constants:

```
const int ConstantValue = 10;
int variableValue = 1;
```

44. Use Nouns to Name Variables

Variables refer to objects or things, which are described by nouns. Pluralize variables that identify collections:

```
public class Customer
{
  private string billingAddress_;
  private string shippingAddress_;
  private string daytimePhone_;
  private Order[] openOrders_;
}
```

45. Add a Prefix or Suffix to Member Variable Names to Distinguish Them from Other Variables

Adopt this practice to reduce the potential for accidental name-hiding and to improve the readability of your code. Choose one style and use it consistently throughout your product. If you are extending or working within a third-party framework, use the same style as the framework. For example, this code uses a trailing underscore to indicate member fields:

```
public class Customer
{
  private string homePhone_;
  private string workPhone_;
}
```

46. Give Constructor and Property Parameters the Same Name as the Fields to Which They Are Assigned

Naming method parameters after the member variables they correspond to provides a clue to the reader that the parameters are assigned to members:

```
public class Customer
{
  private string name_;

  public Customer(string name)
  {
    name_ = name;
  }

  public string Name
  {
    get
    {
      return name_;
    }
  }
}
```

47. Use a Set of Standard Names for "Throwaway" Variables and Parameters

You should use full descriptive names for most variables, but many variable types that appear frequently within C# code have common shorthand names, which you may choose to use instead. The following table lists a few examples:

Loop indices (usually int)	i, j, k
Object	o
String	s
Exception	e or ex
EventArgs	ea
Graphics	g

3.10 Attributes

48. Suffix Custom Attribute Implementations with "Attribute"

It's standard in C# to suffix an attribute class name with "Attribute".

```
public class MyFavoriteAttribute : Attribute
```

Then it is used as:

```
[MyFavorite]
public class Facilitator
```

3.11 Namespaces

49. Use an Organization Name for the Root Namespace, and Narrow by Project, Product, or Group

```
namespace Company.Group.Project
{
  //...
}
```

3.12 Event Handling

50. Clearly Distinguish the Event-Handling Parts Through Appropriate Names

The event class should include a description of the action, such as `MessageReceived`.

The class that raises the event should be a noun. For example, `Messenger`.

The class that defines the data for an event should be something like `MessageReceivedEventArgs`.

A `MessageReceivedEventHandler` is the delegate.

`MessageReceiver` is a class with an `OnMessageReceived()` method which handles a `MessageReceived` event.[11]

3.13 Exceptions

51. *Suffix Custom Exception Types with* Exception

Exceptions are exceptional. Give them an easily-recognizable name.

```
public BadArgumentException : ApplicationException
{
  //...
}
```

---

[11] http://msdn.microsoft.com/library/default.asp?url//library/en-us/cpguide/html/cpconeventsmini-sample.asp.

4.

Documentation

Developers often forget that the primary purpose of their software is to satisfy the needs of an end user; they often concentrate on the solution but fail to instruct others on the use of that solution.

Good software documentation not only tells others how to use your software, but it also acts as a specification of interfaces and behaviors for the engineers who must help you develop the software and those who will later maintain and enhance it. While you should always make every attempt to write software that is self-explanatory, your end users may not have access to the source code, and there will always be significant information about usage and behavior that a programming language cannot express.

Like elegant design and implementation, good documentation is a sign of a professional programmer.

4.1 General

52. Document Your Software Interface for Those Who Must Use It

Document the public interface of your code so others can understand and use it correctly and effectively.

The primary purpose for documentation comments is to define a *programming contract*[12] between a *client* and a supplier of a *service*. The documentation associated with a method should describe all aspects of behavior on which a caller of that method can rely and should not attempt to describe implementation details.

53. Document Your Implementation for Those Who Must Maintain It

Document the implementation of your code so others can maintain and enhance it. Always assume that someone who is completely unfamiliar with your code will eventually have to read and understand it.

54. Keep Your Comments and Code Synchronized

> When the code and the comments disagree, both are probably wrong.
>
> —*Norm Schryer, Bell Labs*

When you modify code, make sure you also update any related comments. The code and documentation together form a software product, so treat each with equal importance.

55. Document Software Elements as Early as Possible

Document each software element before or during its implementation; do not delay until the project is nearing completion. Documentation generated at the end of a project often lacks detail because the authors have become too familiar or too bored with the code.

---

[12] Kernighan, Brian and P. J. Plauger. *The Elements of Programming Style.* (New York: McGraw-Hill, 1988), p. 118.

If you create software reference documentation prior to implementation, you can use this documentation to define requirements for the developers assigned to implement the software.

56. Write for an International Audience

Given the global nature of the software market place, assume that your software will be used internationally. Writing for an international audience means creating documentation that can be read easily by nonnative speakers of your language, and that is easy to translate into other languages if your software is ever localized to other target markets.

Be concise, use simple syntax, and employ a standard, consistent terminology. Minimize the use of acronyms, and avoid idiomatic expressions. Whenever possible, include nonnative speakers on your review list. Use appropriate currency and measurement units. Avoid offensive language.[13]

57. Add Copyright, License, and Author Information to the Top of Every File

Add a header comment block to the top of every source file containing a copyright or license notice. Most computer software contains trade secrets, so you should protect your work from unauthorized copying. Even if your source code will be freely distributed, you should state the terms under which your work may be used, redistributed, or modified.

If you choose to add revision numbers and modification dates to the header comment block, establish a mechanism for keeping this information up-to-date and in sync, such as a

---

[13] http://msdn.microsoft.com/library/default.asp?url=/library/en-us/vbcon/html/vboriInternationalization.asp.

keyword that is expanded by your configuration management system, or standard string that can easily be searched for and replaced.

4.2 API

58. Make Liberal Use of the Documentation Mechanism Built into the C# Language

C# allows you to embed XML comments directing into your source code for the automatic generation of API documentation. Automatically generated documentation is typically more accurate, complete, and up-to-date than externally maintained documentation.

Although the compiler will process any tag that is valid XML, Microsoft provides a list of recommended XML elements. Apply XML comments to all public, protected, and internal declarations. Always include `<summary>` tags, and include `<param>`, `<return>`, and `<exception>` tags where appropriate. Use a `<value>` tag for the data a property gets and sets. Provide `<example>` sections to illustrate common and proper usage, and indicate cross-references using `<see cref=""/>` and `<seealso cref=""/>` tags.

The C# compiler exports the documentation comments in your source code into an XML file, but leaves the final processing of the XML file to you. A common technique is to use XSLT to transform the XML into help files. NDoc[14] is a useful open-source utility that processes .NET assemblies and XML documentation comment files to generate API documentation in several common formats, including MSDN-style HTML Help format (`.chm`), Visual Studio.NET Help format (HTML

---

[14] http://ndoc.sourceforge.net/.

Help 2), MSDN-online style Web pages, and JavaDoc style
Web pages.

59. Document Important Preconditions, Postconditions, and Invariant Conditions

A *precondition* is a condition that must hold true before a
method starts if the method is to behave properly. A typical
precondition may limit the range of acceptable values for a
method parameter.

A *postcondition* is a condition that must hold true following the
completion of a method if this method has behaved properly.
A typical postcondition describes the state of an object that
should result from an invocation of the method given an initial
state and the invocation arguments.

An *invariant* is a condition that must always hold true for
an object. A typical invariant might restrict an integer field
representing the current month to a value between 1 and 12.

Documenting preconditions, postconditions, and invariants
are important because these define the assumptions under
which users interact with a class. For example, if a method
allocates resources that must be released by the caller, then
this should be clearly documented.

See also Rules #75 and #146.

60. Document Thread Synchronization Requirements

If a class or method might be used in a multithreaded environment, document the level of thread safety provided. Indicate
whether the object may be shared between threads and, if so,
whether it requires external synchronization to enforce serialized access. A fully thread-safe object or function uses its
own synchronization mechanism to protect internal state in
the presence of multiple threads.

See also Rule #82.

61. Document Known Defects and Deficiencies

Identify and describe any outstanding problems associated with a class or method. Indicate any replacements or workarounds that exist. If possible, indicate when the problem might be resolved.

While no one likes to publicize problems in his or her code, your colleagues and customers will appreciate the information. This information gives them the chance to implement a workaround or to isolate the problem to minimize the impact of future changes.

62. Use the Active Voice to Describe Actors and Passive Voice to Describe Actions

In English prose, the active voice is normally preferred over the passive voice. However, this is not always the case in technical documentation. This is especially true when a document provides usage instructions.

Use the active voice when the actor in a situation is important.

Prefer:

- *A* Time *object represents a point in time.*
- *Use* Time() *to get the current system time.*

Avoid:

- *A point in time is represented by a* Time *object.*
- *The system time is returned by* Time().

Use the passive voice when the object being acted upon or the action is important but the actor is not:

- *The* Guard *object is destroyed upon exit from the enclosing block scope.*
- *The* Reset() *method must be called prior to invoking any other method.*

You may choose to treat a software element as the implied subject in single-sentence, synoptic descriptions of that element:

```
[Time()] Returns the current time.
```

However, do not use this grammatical style in the main body of the element description. Use complete sentences that identify the element by name or "this" instead:

- *The* Time() *method ignores time zones.*
- *This method ignores time zones.*

63. Use "this" Rather than "the" When Referring to Instances of the Current Class

When describing the purpose or behavior of a method, use "this" instead of "the" to refer to an object that is an instance of the class defining the method:

```
/// <summary>
/// Returns a formatted string representation of
/// this object.
/// </summary>
public override string ToString();
```

4.3 Internal Code

64. Add Internal Comments Only if They Will Aid Others in Understanding Your Code

Avoid the temptation to insert comments that provide useless or irrelevant information:

```
public int OccurrencesOf(Object item)
{
  // This turned out to be much simpler
```

```
  // than I expected.
  return (Find(item) != null) ? 1 : 0;
}
```

Add comments only when they provide information that will help others understand how the code works:

```
public int OccurrencesOf(Object item)
{
  // This works because no duplicates are allowed:
  return (Find(item) != null) ? 1 : 0;
}
```

If an internal comment does not add any value, it is best to let the code speak for itself.

65. *Explain Why the Code Does What It Does*

Good code is self-documenting. Another developer should be able to look at well-written code and determine *what* it does; however, he or she may not know *why* it does it.

The comments in the following code provide little additional information:

```
// Divide the vector components by the vector
// length.
double length = 0;
for (int i = 0; i < vectorCount; i++)
{
  double x = vector[i].x;
  double y = vector[i].y;
  length = Math.Sqrt(x * x, y * y);
  vector[i].x = vector[i].x / length;
  vector[i].x = vector[i].x / length;
}
```

After reading this code, a reasonable developer may still not understand why this code does what it does. Use internal comments to provide this information:

```
// Normalize each vector to produce a unit vector
// which can be used as a direction vector in
// geometry calculations and transformations.
double length = 0;
for (int i = 0; i < vectorCount; i++)
{
  double x = vector[i].x;
  double y = vector[i].y;
  length = Math.Sqrt(x * x, y * y);
  vector[i].x = vector[i].x / length;
  vector[i].x = vector[i].x / length;
}
```

66. Avoid C-style Block Comments

C# supports both C-style block comments delimited by /* and */, as well as one-line comments indicated by //. Avoid the use of C-style block comments. When block comments are large, it is not visually obvious in some editors which lines are commented out. The Block Comment/Uncomment tool in Visual Studio .NET is an easy way to comment out dead code using multiple one-line comments.

67. Use One-Line Comments to Explain Implementation Details

Use one or more one-line comments to document:

- The purpose of specific variables or expressions.
- Any implementation-level design decisions.
- The source material for complex algorithms.
- Defect fixes or workarounds.

- Code that may benefit from further optimization or elaboration.
- Any known problems, limitations, or deficiencies.

Strive to minimize the need for embedded comments by writing code that documents itself. Do not add comments that simply repeat what the code does. Add comments only if they add useful information:

```
// Calculate discount before printing the total.
if (invoiceTotal > DiscountThreshold)
{
  // The discount is hard-coded because current
  // customers all use the same discount rate.
  // We will need to replace this constant with a
  // variable if we ever get a customer who needs
  // a different rate, or one that wants to apply
  // multiple discount rates!
  invoiceTotal *= Discount;
}
```

68. *Avoid the Use of End-Line Comments*

Avoid adding comments to the end of a line of code. Such comments can easily interfere with the visual structure of code. Modifications to a commented line of code may push the comment far enough to the right that it cannot be seen in a text editor. Some programmers try to improve the appearance of end-line comments by aligning them so they are left justified. If this appearance is to be maintained, the comments must be realigned each time the code is modified.

Place one-line comments on a separate line immediately preceding the code to which they refer. There are exceptions to this rule, such as when a comment labels a line of code to identify changes or to support search-and-replace operations. End-of-line comments may also be used to describe simple local variables or to label highly nested control structures (see next rule).

69. Label Closing Braces in Highly Nested Control Structure

While you should generally avoid creating deeply nested control structures, you can improve the readability of such code by adding end-line comments to the closing braces of each structure:

```
for (int i = 0 ...)
{
  for (int j = 0 ...)
  {
    while (! done)
    {
      if (...)
      {
        switch (...)
        {
          //...
        } // end switch
      } // end if
    } // end while
  } // end for j
} // end for i
```

Deeply nested control structures may indicate that refactoring is advisable.

70. Use Keywords to Mark Pending Work, Unresolved Issues, Defects, and Bug Fixes

Establish a set of keywords or tags for use in creating special comments that you and other developers can use to mark and locate important sections of code. These flags are especially useful in marking sections of code that are known to be incomplete or incorrect or require further inspection.

Keywords used to label unresolved issues should include the name or initials of the person who raised the issue and the date that this person identified or resolved the issue. Choose keyword strings that are unlikely to appear anywhere else in the code:

```
// **FIX** - Added code to flush buffer.
// TODO John Smith 5/5/2005
// This code does not handle the case where
// the input overflows the internal buffer!!
while (everMoreInput)
{
  ...
}
```

Some IDEs, such as Visual Studio, can provide automated summaries of such keywords.[15]

71. Label Empty Statements

When a control structure such as a while or for loop has an empty statement by design, add a comment to indicate this was your intent.

```
// Strip leading spaces
while ((c = reader.Read()) == ' ');
// Empty!
```

---

[15] http://msdn.microsoft.com/library/default.asp?url=/library/en-us/vsent7/html/vxconcreatingtaskreminders.asp.

5.

Design

A complete treatment of design principles is clearly beyond the scope of this book. However, this chapter includes some core principles that we have found to be central to good software engineering.

5.1 Engineering

72. Do Not Be Afraid to Do Engineering

The ultimate goal of professional software development is to create something useful—an engineering task much more than a scientific one. (Science is more immediately concerned with understanding the world around us, which is admittedly necessary, but not sufficient, for engineering.)

Resist the temptation to write code to model scientific realities that include all theoretical possibilities. It is not a "hack" to write code that has practical limitations if you are confident those limits do not affect the utility of the resulting system.

For example, imagine you need a data structure for tree traversal and choose to write a stack. The stack needs to hold at least as many items as the maximum depth of any tree. Now suppose that there is no theoretical limit to how deep one of these trees can be. You might be tempted to create a stack that can grow to an arbitrary size by reallocating memory and copying its items as needed. On the other hand, your team's understanding of the application may be such that in your wildest imagination you'd be amazed to see a tree with depth greater than 10. If so, the better choice would be to create a fixed-length stack with a maximum of, say, 50 elements.

You might hear a little voice complain, "There is still a chance greater than zero that a tree will come along with 51 elements and my application will fail, therefore my code is wrong." Be assured, if you write the more complex class to handle any eventuality, there is a much larger chance that your application will fail due to a programming error, unexpected side effects, or misunderstanding of the class's semantics.[16]

This said, it is also important to document any assumptions that you're making and any practical limitations you're aware of. It is very realistic that someone needing a stack will come along later and decide to make use of the one you've already written, but 50 elements might not be a reasonable number of items for that one. This documentation should appear directly in the code, as well as any technical documentation that accompanies the system.

73. *Choose Simplicity Over Elegance*

Strive for elegance in designs and code, but sometimes it is better to stop short of the most elegant solution in favor of a simpler one. While elegant solutions often have an element of simplicity, it is not always the case that simple solutions are elegant. There is nothing particularly elegant about a 50-line sequence of `if-else` statements, but if it is the simplest most straightforward approach to the problem, there is no reason to try and turn it into something it does not need to be.

---

[16] This example is just to illustrate the principle; in this specific case, you'd likely be better off using the classes in the System.Collections namespace. Don't build what you don't have to; see also Rule #74.

74. *Recognize the Cost of Reuse*

Reuse is often held up as the holy grail of object-oriented programming and, indeed, reuse is a wonderful thing for obvious reasons. But do not overlook the costs such as increased dependencies and complexity, which can sometimes outweigh any benefits.

Reusable components are notoriously hard to build and maintain. A designer has to anticipate a wide variety of usage scenarios. Once they are in use, maintenance becomes very difficult due largely to backwards compatibility issues. The assumption that components should be reusable by default also puts stress on development organizations because it forces increased coordination between different groups. More users leads to increased complexity which leads to higher costs.

75. *Program by Contract*

A method is a contract[17] between a caller and a callee. The contract states the caller must abide by the preconditions of the method and the method, in turn, must return results that satisfy the postconditions associated with that method.

Abiding by the preconditions of a method usually means passing arguments as the method expects them; it may also mean calling a set of methods in the correct order. To abide by the postconditions of the method, the method must correctly complete the work it was called upon to perform and it must leave the object in a consistent state.

Check preconditions and postconditions with exceptions and assertions (see Rule #146) in appropriate public methods. Check preconditions at the beginning of a method, before any other code is executed, and check postconditions at the

---

[17] Meyer, Bertrand. *Object-Oriented Software Construction, Second Edition.* (Englewood Cliffs, NJ: Prentice Hall, 2000).

end of a method before the method returns (see also Rule #59).

Derived classes that override superclass methods must preserve the pre- and postconditions of the superclass method. To ensure this, use the template method design pattern[18] by using public non-virtual methods to call protected virtual methods that provide the functional implementation. Each public method will test preconditions, call the associated virtual method, and then test postconditions. A subclass may override public behavior in a superclass by overriding virtual methods:

```csharp
public class LinkedList<T>
{
  public void Prepend(T t)
  {
    // Test precondition
    Debug.Assert(...);

    DoPrepend(t);

    // Test postcondition
    Debug.Assert(Object.Equals(this[0], t));
  }

  protected virtual void DoPrepend(T t)
  {
    ...
  }
}

public class Stack<T>: LinkedList<T>
{
  protected override void DoPrepend(T t)
```

[18] Gamma, Erich, Richard Helm, Ralph Johnson, and John Vlissides. *Design Patterns: Elements of Reusable Object-Oriented Software.* (Reading, Massachusetts: Addison-Wesley, 1994), pp. 325–330.

```
  {
    ...
  }
}
```

76. *Choose an Appropriate Engineering Methodology*

Consider choosing a software design methodology appropriate to your project. Design methodologies standardize best practices and avoid the pitfalls and poor communication that often cause software projects to fail. For example, agile software development is a family of related methodologies that emphasizes small self-organizing teams, iterative development cycles, and continuous testing and integration. Extreme Programming (XP) is a popular member of the agile development family.[19] Agile development differs from "traditional" approaches which emphasize rigorous upfront planning and a document-driven lifecycle.

77. *Separate Distinct Programming Layers*

Separating distinct programming layers creates an architecture that is more flexible and easier to maintain. A three-tier architecture, for example, classically contains three layers: the presentation layer, containing the user interface, the middle layer, containing the application logic, and the data access layer. The presentation layer only communicates with the application layer. The middle layer handles the business logic and in turn communicates with the data access layer. If the data access layer needs to be changed, or even entirely replaced, it can be done without having to modify the presentation layer.

Note that logical layers and physical tiers are not necessarily the same thing.[20]

---

[19] http://www.extremeprogramming.org/.
[20] http://www.lhotka.net/WeBlog/PermaLink.aspx?guid-d9f0d5e8-76ba-4e3b-a60c-a727d0818473.

5.2 Class Design

78. Keep Classes Simple

If you are not sure that a method is required, do not add it. Do not add a method if other methods or a combination thereof can be used to efficiently provide the same functionality. It is much easier to add a method later than to take one out.

See also Martin Fowler's discussion of "Humane Interfaces."[21]

79. Define Derived Classes so They May Be Used Anywhere Their Ancestor Classes May Be Used

A derived class that changes or restricts the behavior of its parent class by overriding something is a *specialization* of that class, but its instances may have limited substitutability for the instances of its ancestor class. It may not always be possible to use the specialization anywhere the parent class could be used.

A derived class that is behaviorally compatible with an ancestor class is a *subtype* and its instances are fully substitutable for instances of its ancestor. A derived class that implements a subtype does not override the behavior of its ancestor class; it only extends the services provided by that class. A subtype has the same attributes and associations as its parent.

The following design principles address the question of substitutability.

The Liskov Substitution Principle

> Methods that use references to superclasses must be able to use objects of subclasses without knowing it. [22]*

---

[21] http://www.martinfowler.com/bliki/HumaneInterface.html.

[22] Liskov, Barbara and John Guttag. *Abstraction and Specification in Program Development.* (New York: McGraw-Hill, 1986).

* This is our interpretation of Barbara Liskov's original formulation: "*If for each object O1 of type S there is an object O2 of type T such that for all programs P defined*

According to this principle, the ability to substitute a derived object for a parent object is characteristic of good design. Such designs offer more stability and reliability when compared with designs that fail to uphold this principle. When a design adheres to this principle, it generally indicates the designer did a good job identifying the base abstractions and generalizing their interfaces.

The Open-Closed Principle

> Software entities, i.e. classes, modules, functions, and so forth, should be open for extension, but closed for modification.[23,24]

Any design that requires code changes to handle the introduction of a newly derived class is a bad design. Whenever a derived class violates the existing contract between its ancestors and their clients, it forces changes in the existing code. When a method accepts an ancestor instance, yet uses the derived type of this instance to control its behavior, changes are required for the introduction of each new subclass. Changes of this kind violate the *Open-Closed Principle* and are something to avoid.

Consider the following example:

```
public abstract class Shape
{
  public abstract void Resize(double scale);
}

public class Rectangle : Shape
```

---

in terms of T, the behavior of P is unchanged when O1 is substituted for O2, then S is a subtype of T."

[23] Martin, Robert. "Engineering Notebook: The Open-Closed Principle," C++ Report, Vol. 8, No. 1 (Jan 1996).

[24] Martin, Robert "Engineering Notebook," C++ Report, Vol. 8, No. 3 (Mar 1996).

```csharp
{
  protected double width_;
  protected double height_;

  public double Width
  {
    get
    {
      return width_;
    }
    set
    {
      width_ = value;
    }
  }

  public double Height
  {
    get
    {
      return height_;
    }
    set
    {
      height_ = value;
    }
  }

  public override void Resize(double scale)
  {
    this.Width *= scale;
    this.Height *= scale;
  }
}
```

These classes form part of a simple hierarchy of shapes for a hypothetical drawing package. A Rectangle is described in terms of width and height. The Resize() method is used to simultaneously scale the width and height of a Rectangle.

Now suppose you decide that you want to add a new class to represent squares. A square is simply a specialized form of rectangle, so you create a class called Square that derives from Rectangle:

```
public class Square : Rectangle
{
  public double Size
  {
    get
    {
      return width_;
    }
    set
    {
      width_ = value;
      height_ = value;
    }
  }
}
```

Since squares have identical width and height, you have added a Size property that always gives the width and height the same value on set. However, this implementation has a problem; if a Square is passed as a Rectangle to another software entity that sets either the Width or Height properties, the result might be a Square that no longer satisfies the width == height constraint. This behavior violates the *Liskov Substitution Principle*.

You might think to solve this problem by converting Width and Height into virtual properties and overriding those properties in Square to guarantee satisfaction of the constraint:

```csharp
public class Rectangle : Shape
{
  ...
  public virtual double Width
  {
    get
    {
      return width_;
    }
    set
    {
      width_ = value;
    }
  }

  public virtual double Height
  {
    get
    {
      return height_;
    }
    set
    {
      height_ = value;
    }
  }
  ...
}

public class Square : Rectangle
{
  public override double Width
  {
    get
    {
      return width_;
    }
```

```
  set
  {
    width_ = value;
    height_ = value;
  }
}
public override double Height
{
  get
  {
    return height_;
  }
  set
  {
    width_ = value;
    height_ = value;
  }
}
}
```

While this change solves the problem described above, it required modification of the Rectangle parent, which you may or may not have the permission to change. Because this solution required changes in existing code, it violates the *Open-Closed Principle*.

The *Liskov Substitution* and *Open-Closed Principles* also apply to methods. In the following example, the DrawShape() method in the Canvas class would have to be modified to handle a new shape class, such as Square:

```
public class Canvas
{
  public void DrawShape(Shape shape)
  {
    // Use derived type to call relevant method
```

```
    if (shape is Circle)
    {
      DrawCircle(shape as Circle);
    }
    else if (shape is Rectangle)
    {
      DrawRectangle(shape as Rectangle);
    }
  }

  public void DrawCircle(Circle circle) {...}

  public void DrawRectangle(Rectangle rect) {...}
}
```

A developer would have to change the Canvas class and the DrawShape() method each time they wanted to add a new subclass of the Shape class. Solve this problem by adding a DrawSelf() method to the Shape subclasses and replacing the shape-specific methods on the canvas with a set of primitive drawing operations that Shape objects can use to draw themselves.[25] Each subclass of Shape would override the DrawSelf() method to call the canvas drawing operations necessary to produce that particular shape:

```
public abstract class Shape
{
  ...
  public abstract void DrawSelf(Canvas canvas);
  ...
}

public class Circle : Shape
{
  ...
```

---

[25] Also known as "double-dispatch." See Erich Gamma et al. *Design Patterns: Elements of Reusable Object-Oriented Software.* (Reading, Massachusetts, Addison-Wesley, 1994), pp. 338–339.

```
  public override void DrawSelf(Canvas canvas)
  {...}
  ...
}

public class Canvas
{
  ...
  public void DrawShapes(IEnumerable<Shape>
                          shapes)
  {
    foreach(Shape shape in shapes)
    {
      shape.DrawSelf(this);
    }
  }

  // Define the operations the shapes will use
  public void DrawLine(int x1,int y1,int x2,int y2)
  {...}

  public void DrawCircle(int x, int y, int radius)
  {...}
  ...
}
```

80. Use Inheritance for is-a Relationships and Containment for has-a Relationships

Making a choice between inheritance and containment is one of the most important decisions to be made in producing an object-oriented design. As a rule of thumb, use inheritance to model *is-a* relationships, and containment to model *has-a* relationships.

For example, a truck *has-a* set of wheels and an ice-cream truck *is-a* specialized kind of truck:

```
public class Wheel
```

```
{
  ...
}

public class Truck
{
  private Wheel[] wheels_;
}

public class IceCreamTruck : Truck
{
  ...
}
```

81. Use Abstract Base Classes for "is-a" Relationships and Interfaces for "implements" Relationships

As a rule of thumb, use a base class to specify *is-a* relationships between classes, and interfaces to specify *implements* relationships.

When choosing between classes and interfaces, keep in mind:

- Classes can contain fields and default implementations of methods; interfaces can only define method signatures.
- Classes are easier to evolve than interfaces: new members can be added to classes without breaking derived types, while additions to an interface break existing types that implement that interface.
- Classes can have only one base type, while they can implement any number of interfaces.

For a detailed discussion of these factors, see *Framework Design Guidelines.*[26]

---

[26] Cwalina, Krzysztof and Brad Abrams. *Framework Design Guidelines: Conventions, Idioms, and Patterns for Reusable. NET Libraries.* Addison-Wesley, 2005. ISBN 0321246756.

5.3 Thread Safety and Concurrency

Concurrency exists when two or more threads make progress, executing instructions at the same time. A single processor system can simulate concurrency by switching execution between two or more threads. A multiprocessor system can support parallel concurrency by executing a separate thread on each processor.

Many applications can benefit from the use of concurrency in their implementation. In a concurrent model of execution, an application is divided into two or more processes or threads, each executing in its own sequence of statements or instructions. An application may consist of one or more processes and a process may consist of one or more threads. Execution may be distributed among two or more machines in a network, two or more processors in a single machine, or interleaved on a single processor.

The separately executing processes or threads must generally compete for access to shared resources and data and must cooperate to accomplish their overall task.

Concurrent application development is a complicated task. Designing a concurrent application involves determining the necessary number of processes or threads, their particular responsibilities, and the methods by which they interact. It also involves determining the good, legal, or invariant program states and the bad or illegal program states. The critical problem is to find and implement a solution that maintains or guarantees good program states while prohibiting bad program states, even in those situations where two or more threads may be acting on the same resource.

In a concurrent environment, a programmer maintains desirable program states by limiting or negotiating access to shared resources using *synchronization*. The principal role of synchronization is to prevent undesirable or unanticipated interference between simultaneously executing instruction sequences.

Synchronization describes the set of mechanisms or processes for preventing undesirable interleaving of operations or interference between concurrent threads. This is primarily accomplished by serializing access to a shared program state. A programmer may choose between one of two synchronization techniques: *mutual exclusion* or *conditional synchronization.*

Mutual exclusion involves combining fine-grained atomic actions into coarse-grained actions and arranging to make these composite actions atomic.

Condition synchronization describes a process or mechanism that delays the execution of a thread until the program satisfies some predicate or condition.

A thread that is waiting on a synchronization mechanism is said to be *blocked.* Once a thread is *unblocked, awakened,* or *notified,* it is rescheduled for further execution.

Two basic uses exist for thread synchronization: to protect the integrity of shared data and to communicate changes in program state between cooperating threads.

An entity is *multithread-safe (MT-safe)* if multiple threads can simultaneously access that entity. Static class methods may support a different level of thread safety than those associated with an instance of that class. A class or method is considered *multithread-hot (MT-hot)* if it creates additional threads to accomplish its task.

82. Design for Reentrancy

Always write code that is *reentrant,* that is, code that operates correctly when invoked recursively by a single thread or concurrently by multiple threads. To write reentrant code, do not use statically allocated resources unless you use some form of mutual exclusion to guarantee serialized access to that resource. Examples of static resources include shared objects, I/O devices, and other hardware resources.

83. Use Threads Only Where Appropriate

Multithreading does not necessarily equate to improved application performance. Some applications are not suited for multithreading and may run slower following the introduction of multiple threads because of the overhead required to manage those threads.

Before you multithread your application, determine whether it can benefit from their use. Use threads if your application needs[27]:

- To simultaneously respond to many events—for example, a Web browser or server.
- To provide a high level of responsiveness—for example, a user interface implementation that can continue to respond to user actions even while the application is performing other computations.
- To take advantage of machines with multiple processors.

84. Avoid Unnecessary Synchronization

Synchronization can be expensive. Synchronization serializes access to an object thereby minimizing potential concurrency. Before synchronizing code, consider whether that code accesses shared state information. If a method only operates on independently synchronized objects, local variables, or non-volatile data members, such as those initialized during construction, then synchronization is not required.

---

[27] Lea, Doug. *Concurrent Programming in Java*™ : *Design Principles and Patterns.* (Reading, Massachusetts: Addison-Wesley, 1997), pp. 1–2.

Do not synchronize fundamental data types or structures, such as lists, vectors, etc. Let the users of these objects determine whether external synchronization is necessary.

5.4 Efficiency

85. *Use Lazy Evaluation and Initialization*

Do not perform a complex calculation until you need the result. Always perform calculations at the most nested scope possible. If possible, cache the result.

This concept can be applied to object construction and initialization as well—do not construct an object that you may not use until you need it. Access the object using a simple dedicated function. This function must construct the object the first time you call it and return a reference to the object from that point on. Any code that requires access to the object must use that function. Serialization (locking) may be required to prevent concurrent initialization. In the following example, we assume that a LoanCalculator is an object we do not want to build unless we have to:

```
public class LoanCalculator
{
  //...
}

public class PersonalFinance
{

  private LoanCalculator loanCalculator_ = null;

  public double CalculateInterest()
  {
    // Use double-check pattern to prevent
    // concurrent construction
    if (loanCalculator_ == null)
```

```
  {
    // Acquire lock here...
    if (loanCalculator_ == null)
    {
      loanCalculator_ = new LoanCalculator();
    }
      // Release lock here...
  }
  return loanCalculator_.CalculateInterest();
  }
}
```

86. *Reuse Objects to Avoid Reallocation*

Cache and reuse frequently created objects that have limited life spans.

Use accessor methods instead of constructors to reinitialize the object.

Use a factory implementation to encapsulate mechanisms for caching and reusing objects. To manage these mechanisms properly, you must return objects obtained from an object factory back to the same factory. This means that the association between an object and its factory must be maintained somewhere:

- In the class—a single static factory is associated with the class of the object, and that factory manages all objects of that class.
- In the object—the object maintains a reference to the factory that manages it.
- In the owner of the object—an "owner" of an object maintains a reference to the factory from which the object was obtained.

Take care to choose an implementation that does not need to create its own objects to manage the objects being cached. This would defeat the purpose!

87. Leave Optimization for Last

First Rule of Optimization:

> Do not do it.

Second Rule of Optimization (For experts only):

> Do not do it yet.
> —*Michael Jackson, Michael Jackson Systems Ltd.*

Do not spend time optimizing code until you are sure you need to do it.

Apply the 80–20 rule[28]: 20 percent of the code in a system uses 80 percent of the resources (on average). If you are going to optimize, make sure you start with code in the 20 percent portion.

88. Avoid Creating Unnecessary Objects

This is especially important if the new objects have short life spans or are constructed, but never referenced. This not only wastes execution time to create the object, but it also uses time during garbage collection.

Redundant initialization, as illustrated in the following code, is quite common, and wasteful:

```
public Color TextColor
{
  get
  {
```

---

[28] McConnell, Steve. *Code Complete*. (Redmond, Washington: Microsoft Press, 1993), pp. 682–683.

```
    Color c = new Color(...);
    if (this.state < 2)
    {
      c = new Color(...);
    }
    return c;
  }
}
```

Avoid creating an object until you know what you want:

```
public Color TextColor
{
  get
  {
    Color c = null;
    if (this.state < 2)
    {
      c = new Color(...);
    }
    else
    {
      c = new Color(...);
    }
    return c;
  }
}
```

89. *Let the CLR Handle Garbage Collection*

The garbage collector in the Common Language Runtime frees you from tracking memory usage and knowing when to free memory. In general, avoid calling the GC.Collect() method and allow the garbage collector to run independently. In most cases, the garbage collector's optimizing engine is better at determining the best time to perform a collection than you are.

6.

Programming

This chapter describes recommended C# programming conventions.

6.1 Types

90. Use the Built-in C# Datatype Aliases

All primitive types in C# have aliases. For example, `int` is an alias for `System.Int32`. It's best, for readability reasons, to use the alias; that is, instead of:

```
System.Int32 i = new System.Int32(4);
```

write the equivalent, but less cumbersome:

```
int i = 4;
```

91. Avoid Using Inline Literals

Avoid code like this:

```
if (size > 45)
{
  // ...
}
```

Declaring a constant provides improved readability and a single location for changes:

```
const int Limit = 45;
...
```

```
if (size > Limit)
{
  //...
}
```

92. *Avoid Unnecessary Boxing of Value Types*

The conversion of a value type to a reference type is called *boxing* and happens implicitly when you write code like this:

```
object obj = 4;
```

Unboxing is the opposite conversion of a reference type to a value type, like this:

```
int i = (int) obj;
```

If you use a value type in a reference type context, then boxing/unboxing will be required. This comes at a significant performance cost, so when possible, strive to avoid repetitive boxing/unboxing. For example, if you want to store a list of integers, use List instead of the object-based ArrayList.

93. *Write Floating Point Literals in Standard Form*

Floating point numbers should have digits before and after the decimal point.

It's painful to read:

```
const double Foo = 0.042e2;
```

This would at least be standard:

```
const double Foo = 4.2e0;
```

But this is much better:

```
const double Foo = 4.2;
```

94. Use Structs for Value Semantics

In many cases, you can design an object as a `class` or a `struct`. Choosing a `struct` means that the object will be created on the stack with value semantics.

Note that `structs` cannot be derived from a base class, are sealed (so they cannot be derived from), and do not have default constructors.

95. Consider Overriding Equality Methods and Operators on Structs

A `struct` should follow value semantics. Therefore, override the equality methods and operators and implement value behavior rather than inheriting reference behavior from `System.Object`.

96. Use the "@" Prefix to Escape Entire Strings

It's convenient and more readable to use the "@" character to escape all the characters in a string.

```
string path = "c:\\My Folder\\Acme";
```

The previous line can be implemented as a string literal:

```
string path = @"c:\My Folder\Acme";
```

97. Avoid Costly Hidden String Allocations

If this line were in a loop, two string allocations would be required during each iteration.

```
if (str1.ToUpperCase() == str2.ToUpperCase())
```

This cost can easily be avoided by:

```
if (String.Compare(str1, str2, true))
```

Similarly, concatenation of strings requires a string allocation.

```
string str = "";
while ( ... )
{
  str += ".";
}
```

It's much more efficient to use the StringBuilder class and convert to a string when concatenation is complete. In addition, if strings are reused then they should be created as a string.

```
StringBuilder buffer = new StringBuilder();
string temp = ".";
while ( ... )
{
  buffer.Append(temp);
}
string str = buffer.ToString();
```

This approach saves additional string allocations from occurring each iteration.

98. Use an Efficient Check for Empty Strings

A line of code such as:

```
if (str.Equals(""))
```

requires that an empty string be constructed. Checking the length, however, does not:

```
if (str.Length == 0)
```

Furthermore, .NET 2.0 introduced a static method String.IsNullOrEmpty() that checks for both null references and empty strings in one efficient test.

99. Use Nullable Values Only Where Required

Nullable values have been introduced with .NET 2.0. They allow you to have built-in data types that can be set to null.

For example,

```
int? a = null;
```

Although `int?` will work anywhere you have `int`, there's a performance impact to using nullable types, so you shouldn't make this change without a good reason. Only use nullable values if you are certain that you need to have a null value.

100. Use Partial Types Only to Support Machine-Generated Code

Partial classes were introduced into .NET 2.0 primarily to support code generation tools. While code generation is a very useful technique, splitting the non-generated portions of a class into multiple files can be confusing to those reading the code.

6.2 Statements and Expressions

101. Do Not Rely on Operator Precedence in Complex Expressions

Complex expressions are difficult to visually parse and understand, especially those that rely on operator precedence for subexpression evaluation and ordering. You and any future maintainers can easily make mistakes when coding or modifying expressions that rely on operator precedence. Use parentheses to define and control the evaluation of subexpressions. This makes your code easier to understand and easier to maintain:

```
// Trying to get 60
int j = 10 * 2 << 1 + 20;   // Bad! j == 41943040
// Add some parentheses ...
j = (10 * (2 << 1)) + 20;   // Good! j == 60
```

102. Do Not Test for Equality with True or False

It's unnecessary to compare a boolean with false or true.

```
bool b = false;
if (b == false)
{
  // ...
}
```

Use the boolean directly:

```
bool b = false;
if (!b)
{
  // ...
}
```

103. Replace Repeated, Nontrivial Expressions with Equivalent Methods

As you write code, look for repeated expressions or operations that might be factored into separate methods.

When you replace factored code with a function call, you simplify and reduce the size of the code. This makes your code easier to read.

When you replace factored code with a meaningful function name, you improve the self-documenting quality of your code. This makes your code easier to understand.

When you factor code into a single method, you simplify testing, by localizing behavior, and maintenance, by localizing change.

104. Avoid Complex Statements in Ternary Conditions

The ternary form is a convenient, readable control-flow mechanism for simple situations:

```
short i = (d < 0) ? -1 : 1;
```

Don't use it for complex ones:

```
Customer customer = (!busy || flag == 3) ?
  Find(name) :
  CreateCustomer(name, address, birthdate);
```

105. Use `Object.Equals()` *to Test for Object Identity of Reference Types*

The nonstatic `Equals()` method and the `==` operator on a type might have been overridden by a type to use value identity. If you want reference identity then explicitly check for it using `Object.Equals()`.

```
if (Object.Equals(string1, string2))
{
  // ...
}
```

6.3 Control Flow

When we look at a piece of code, we usually begin with the assumption that the statements within that code are executed sequentially. While control flow statements may select different statements or blocks of statements for execution, we still expect control flow to enter a block at the first statement and exit the block after the last—we assume that each block has a single entry and exit point. The software development community has long considered it good programming practice to write code that follows this model. Code written in this manner is often easier to debug because we need only look for a single exit point instead of many.

A C# programmer can subvert this model of control flow by using the goto, break, continue, return, and throw statements. While many situations exist where use of these statements is recommended or even mandatory, these statements are often used in a manner that makes code harder to read, understand, test, and maintain.

106. Avoid break *and* continue *in Iteration Statements*

The break and continue statements interrupt the normal flow of execution. The break statement immediately exits the nearest enclosing iteration statement and all intervening blocks and resumes execution in the statement that follows. The continue statement immediately jumps to the controlling expression of the nearest enclosing iteration statement, exiting all intervening blocks. Both statements produce behavior similar to that of the goto statement.

A reader can easily overlook occurrences of these statements if the enclosing iteration block is large or complex. A reader might also pair a break or continue with the wrong iteration statement and thereby misinterpret the code. Blocks that have multiple exit points are more difficult to debug since a separate breakpoint may be required at each exit point.

Try using a combination of if..else statements and controlling expressions to produce the behavior that you might otherwise get if you used break and continue. However, you may choose to ignore this rule if you find that you must create and evaluate a number of additional state variables or complex expressions just to avoid use of these statements.[29] The cost in complexity and performance may override style considerations. If you do choose to use break or continue statements, add obvious comments to highlight these special exit points.

---

[29] McConnell, Steve. *Code Complete.* (Redmond, Washington: Microsoft Press, 1993), pp. 337–338.

107. *Avoid Multiple* return *Statements in Methods*

When used anywhere but the last statement in a function block, a `return` statement also interrupts normal execution flow. A reader typically looks for the return statement at the end of a function, so if you place them in other locations, add obvious comments to highlight these other exit points.

108. *Do Not Use* goto

The use of `goto` is one of the great religious arguments in computer programming, originally brought to the forefront by Edsger Dijkstra's famous essay, "Go To Statement Considered Harmful."[30]

While `goto` statements may have a place in programming languages without powerful control constructs, suffice it to say that if you think that you need to use a `goto` in C#, you may be doing something wrong[31] (but sometimes not[32]).

109. *Do Not Use* try...throw...catch *to Manage Control Flow*

Whenever possible, you should only use the C# exception mechanism to handle exceptional conditions. Do not use it as a substitute for conditional expressions `if..else`, `for`, `while`, and `do..while` or control flow statements such as `return`, `break`, and `continue`.

See also the "TryParse" pattern.[33]

---

[30] Dijkstra, Edsger W. "Go To Statement Considered Harmful," Communications of the ACM, Vol. 11, No. 3 (Mar 1968), pp. 147–148.

[31] Budd, Timothy. *C++ for Java Programmers*. (Reading, Massachusetts: Addison-Wesley, 1999), pp. 209–210.

[32] McConnell, Steve. *Code Complete*. (Redmond, Washington: Microsoft Press, 1993), section 16.1, pp. 347–359.

[33] http://blogs.msdn.com/kcwalina/archive/2005/03/16/396787.aspx.

110. *Declare For-Loop Iteration Variables Inside of* for *Statements*

Iteration variables should be declared inside a for statement. This limits the scope of the variable to the for statement:

```
for (int count = 0; count < length; count++)
{
  // count is only visible inside this block...
}
```

111. *Add a Default Case Label to the End of All Switch Statements*

Explain how the default case is or is not reached.

```
switch (color)
{
  case Color.Red:
    // ...
    break;
  case Color.Blue:
    // ...
    break;
  case Color.Green:
    // ...
    break;
  default:
    // This should be unreachable, since we're
    // assuming color is only Red, Blue, or Green.
    Debug.Assert(false, "Invalid color value");
}

switch(day)
{
  case Day.Saturday:
    // ...
    break;
```

```
case Day.Sunday:
  // ...
  break;
default:
  // It's a weekday ...
}
```

6.4 Classes

112. Define Small Classes and Small Methods

Smaller classes and methods are easier to design, code, test, document, read, understand, and use. Because smaller classes generally have fewer methods and represent simpler concepts, their interfaces tend to exhibit better cohesion.

Try to limit the interface of each class to the bare minimum number of methods required to provide the necessary functionality. Avoid the temptation to add "convenience" forms of a method when only one general-purpose form suffices.

All sorts of informal guidelines exist for establishing the maximum size of a class or method—use your best judgment. If a class or method seems too big, then consider refactoring that class or method into additional classes or methods. Do not hesitate to factor a large method into smaller, private methods even if you only call these smaller methods once from within another method. The subdivided code will be easier to understand, and you might yet discover that you can reuse some of the new methods. In addition, the CLR can optimize code better if it is broken into smaller methods.

113. Build Fundamental Classes from Standard Types

When designing low-level fundamental or concrete types, you should strive to minimize dependencies on non-standard types. Every time you include a non-standard type in the interface of a fundamental type, you introduce a new and potentially volatile dependency. Such dependencies may not only make your code more susceptible to change, but also increases the compilation and execution "footprint" of that code.

Limit yourself to the types defined in .NET whenever possible.

114. Avoid the Use of Virtual Base Classes in User-Extensible Class Hierarchies

A user that extends a class hierarchy that possesses virtual base classes may not be aware that they may need to invoke a virtual parent constructor in the constructors of derived classes. If you expect users to extend a class that has a virtual base class, you need to fully describe if and how they must initialize the parent, perhaps forcing you to reveal implementation details that might have best remained hidden.

If you must use virtual parent classes, try to design your implementation such that the virtual parent can be initialized using a default constructor—the compiler automatically invokes this constructor if the user fails to specify one.

115. Declare the Access Level of All Members

Do not assume that others will remember the default access level. When possible, group declarations into a single section for each access level. Many programmers declare sections in the following order: `public`, followed by `protected`, followed by `private`.

116. Mark Classes Sealed to Prevent Unwanted Derivation

If you want to prohibit derivation from a "closed" class, use the `sealed` keyword. All access modifiers should be `public` or `private`; `protected` doesn't make any sense in this context.

```
public sealed class ClosedClass
{
  private int id;

  public ClosedClass()
  {
    // ...
  }
}

// Illegal! Cannot derive from a sealed class!
public class Derived : ClosedClass
{
  // ...
}
```

Significant debate exists in the programming community about the wisdom of using the `sealed` keyword.[34]

117. Avoid the Use of `internal` Declarations

Internal declarations are often indicative of poor design because they bypass access restrictions and hide dependencies between classes and functions. You should only use them when you want to prevent a subclass from gaining access to certain superclass methods while allowing certain helper classes, operators, and functions to access those same methods.

118. Avoid the Use of `new` to Hide Members of a Derived Type

If a subclass has a function with the same signature as its parent, but yet the function is not overriding a virtual function, then

---

[34] http://www.sellsbrothers.com/news/showTopic.aspx?ixTopic=411.

you may have a faulty design. Using the new keyword simply to work around compiler errors should be avoided.

119. Limit the Use of Base to Subclass Constructors and Overridden Methods

The base keyword can be used to call any function on a base class. It should be used only where necessary; for example:

```
public Child() : base()
{
  // ...
}
public override object Clone()
{
  Foo foo = (Foo) base.Clone();
  foo.field = field;
  return foo;
}
```

The use of base here is confusing:

```
public bool IsGood()
{
  // Just call Solve()
  return (base.Solve() != null);
}
```

120. Override operator == and operator! = When Overriding the Equals() Method

It's clearer if the equality operators stay in sync with the Equals() method.

```
public boolean operator==(Student lhs,
                          Student rhs)
```

```
{
  return lhs == null?
    rhs == null : lhs.Equals(rhs);
}

public bool Equals(Student rhs)
{
  return ((rhs != null) && (id_ == rhs.id_));
}
```

121. Consider Overriding the Implicit String Conversion Operator When Overriding the ToString() Method

Overriding the ToString() method with a meaningful string representation of a class can be very helpful for debugging and logging purposes.

If explicit conversion to string makes sense, perhaps implicit conversion would be useful as well. However, if you do this, be aware that your type can then be used anywhere a string can, which may have unintended consequences.

122. Implement a Method in Terms of Its Opposite

Implementing one method in terms of its opposite is consistent with two goals: making the meaning of a method obvious (see Rule #2), and simplifying code:

```
public void Deposit(double amount)
{
  balance_ += amount;
}

public void Withdraw(double amount)
{
  Deposit(-amount);
}
```

It is logical for a reader of your code to expect that `Deposit()` would be consistent with the logical negation of `Withdraw()`; when you implement methods in this way, you guarantee those semantics, even if the implementation of one changes at a later date. The same could be said for `operator+` and `operator-`, for example.

6.5 Life Cycle

123. Initialize All Variables

The uninitialized variable is one of the most common and insidious of all software defects. Software containing an uninitialized variable may work only because its memory location happens to contain a viable value. This may hold true for years, until a new compilation or invocation order results in code that leaves a different, unexpected value in the variable's memory location.

The risk of this occurring is greatly reduced in a managed code environment like the CLR: in most cases, failing to initialize a variable leads to a compiler error.[35] It's good practice, and most readable, to get in the habit of explicitly initializing all variables that you use.

124. Always Construct Objects in a Valid State

Never allow an invalid object to be constructed. If you implement a constructor that does not produce a valid object because you intend to use it as part of a multistage initialization process, make that constructor protected or private and use a static method to coordinate the construction.

---

[35] Except for instance variables; see http://www.cookcomputing.com/blog/archives/000403.html.

To keep your constructors simple and fast, consider using lazy evaluation to delay initialization (see Rule #85).

125. Declare an Explicit Default Constructor for Added Clarity and COM Interoperability

You should declare and implement a public default constructor to make it clear that your class supports default construction. You should define one even if there are no initializers and the function body is empty. If you allow the compiler to generate the constructor, you may fail to consider all of the initialization requirements for your class. When you supply a default constructor you provide source code that can be used for setting debug breakpoints and execution tracing.

You should declare a protected default constructor if your class does not support default construction. Directly instantiating a default instance would produce a compilation error. You only need to provide an implementation for a protected constructor if you want to provide default construction functionality to subclasses (see also Rule #126).

You should declare a private default constructor if your class does not support default construction or consists only of static members. Directly instantiating a default instance would produce a compilation error. You do not need to provide an implementation in this case since the constructor will never be invoked.

Note also that if you provide any other constructors, the compiler does not generate a default constructor for you.

126. Make Constructors Protected to Prohibit Direct Instantiation

To prohibit direct instantiation of an abstract class, you should only allow protected access to all of its constructors. Derived classes will still be able to construct the abstract class, but other entities will not.

127. Always List Any Base Constructors in the Initializer List of a Derived Constructor

A derived class should not directly initialize a parent member—parent member initialization is the responsibility of the parent constructor. Instead, always include the appropriate parent constructor in the initializer list, even if it is a default constructor:

```
public class Base
{
  protected int foo_;

  public Base(int foo)
  {
    foo_ = foo;
  }
}
public class A : Base
{
  public A(int foo)
  {
    // Bad! Let Base() do this!
    foo_ = foo;
  }
}
public class B : Base
{
  public B(int foo) : base(foo) // Good!
  {
  }
}
```

128. Use Nested Constructors to Eliminate Redundant Code

To avoid writing redundant constructor code, call lower-level constructors from higher-level constructors.

This code implements the same low-level initialization in two different places:

```
public class Account
{
  private string name_;
  private double balance_;
  const double DefaultBalance = 0.0d;

  public Account(string name, double balance)
  {
    name_ = name;
    balance_ = balance;
  }

  public Account(string name)
  {
    name_ = name;
    balance_ = DefaultBalance;
  }
}
```

This code implements the low-level initialization in one place only:

```
public class Account
{
  private string name_;
  private double balance_;
  const double DefaultBalance = 0.0d;

  public Account(string name, double balance)
  {
    name_ = name;
```

```
    balance_ = balance;
  }
  public Account(string name)
  {
    this(name, DefaultBalance);
  }
}
```

This approach is also helpful if you are using assertions, as it typically reduces the number of places a given constructor argument appears, thus reducing the number of places the validity of that argument is checked.

129. Implement IDisposable on Classes Referencing External Resources

Always invoke Dispose() or Close() on classes that offer it.

Always implement the IDisposable interface and pattern if your class has external or unmanaged resources.

Provide the Dispose() method from IDisposable, and call your custom finalization code.[36] Suppress .NET garbage collection in this case.

```
public void Dispose()
{
  Dispose(true);
  GC.SuppressFinalize(this);
}
```

Implement a protected method to do the cleanup:

```
protected void Dispose(bool disposing)
{
```

---

[36] See "Nondeterministic Destruction" in Jeff Prosise's *Programming Microsoft .NET* (Microsoft Press, 2002), pp. 38–42, for an excellent explanation of this pattern.

```
    // Check if already called.
    if(! disposed_)
  {
    // If disposing equals true, dispose all
    // managed and unmanaged resources.
    if(disposing)
    {
      // Dispose managed resources.
    }

    // Call the appropriate methods to clean up
    // unmanaged resources here.
    disposed_ = true;
  }
}
```

See also Rule #150.

6.6 Fields and Properties

130. Declare All Fields with Private Access, and Use Properties to Provide Access

Declare all class data members (known as *fields* in C#) with private access, and use *properties* to give class users and derived classes access to those private data members. Treat the implementation details as private information to reduce the impact on dependent classes should the implementation change, and to allow data to be validated consistently.

The following code provides read and write access to the private month field:

```
class Date
{
  private int month_;
```

```
  public int Month
  {
    get
    {
      return month_;
    }
    set
    {
      month_ = value;
    }
  }
}
```

If class users should be able to read the month value but not change it, the set property can be omitted:

```
class Date
{
  private int month_;

  public int Month
  {
    get
    {
      return month_;
    }
  }
}
```

Data validation can be included in the property implementation; in this way, all modifications to the property will be validated consistently:

```
class Date
{
  private int month_;

  public int Month
```

```
  {
    get
    {
      return month_;
    }
    set
    {
      if (value < 1 || value > 12)
      {
        throw new ArgumentOutOfRangeException();
      }
      month_ = value;
    }
  }
}
```

131. Use Properties Only for Simple, Inexpensive, Order-Independent Access

To API consumers, properties look like data fields and are often treated as such. Accordingly, the implementation of a property should not be computationally expensive or have unexpected side effects.

For example, it is appropriate for a property to return the value of a private member or perform a simple calculation; it is probably not appropriate for a set property to save information to a database or for a get property to download a Web page. Such operations should be exposed as explicit methods so that the effect is clear to the caller.

6.7 Methods

132. Avoid Passing an Excessive Number of Parameters

If a method takes a very large number of parameters, consider whether it should be redesigned. Many parameters might indicate that a single method is doing too much, or that several related parameters might be further abstracted behind another class.

Code like this:

```
public bool IsPolicyValid(int originalYear,
                          int originalMonth,
                          int originalDay,
                          int originalHour,
                          int renewalYear,
                          int renewalMonth,
                          int renewalDay,
                          int renewalHour,
                          int effectiveYear,
                          int effectiveMonth,
                          int effectiveDay,
                          int effectiveHour)
{
  //...
}
```

might be better rewritten with a Date abstraction like this:

```
public bool IsPolicyValid(DateTime originalDate,
                          DateTime renewalDate,
                          DateTime effectiveDate)
{
  //...
}
```

133. Validate Parameter Values

If a method makes any assumptions about the values of its parameter (for example, an integer representing a month is between 1 and 12), validate the parameters at the beginning of the method.

Depending on the desired runtime behavior, and whether validation should be performed in both release and debug builds, you might use the features in the System. Diagnostics.Debug class or throw an exception in the System.Exception class hierarchy. See also Rules #148 and #158.

6.8 Attributes

134. Deprecate APIs Using System.ObsoleteAttribute

If an interface changes between releases of a class library, deprecate the old interface using System.ObsoleteAttribute rather than simply removing or changing the interface. This allows a compile-time message to be displayed to consumers of the class that explains the change and perhaps suggests a workaround.

One constructor for System.ObsoleteAttribute allows the class implementer to specify whether continued use of the deprecated element is permitted (a compiler warning) or not (a compiler error).

135. Consider Whether New Classes Should Be Serializable

Consider whether new classes should be serializable. Refer to "Serialization Guidelines" in the Microsoft .NET Framework Developer's Guide[37] for factors to consider (including security) when making this decision about a given class.

---

[37] http://msdn.microsoft.com/library/default.asp?url=library/en-us/cpguide/html/cpconserializationguidelines.asp.

There are multiple ways to make a class serializable: marking the class with the `Serializable` attribute is easiest, since it doesn't require additional code. Alternatively, implementing the `ISerializable` interface can result in higher performance, since it doesn't use reflection like the `Serializable` approach does, and also allows more control over the output.

136. Use the `System.FlagsAttribute` to Designate Bitfields

Marking an enumeration with `System.FlagsAttribute` indicates to the compiler that the values can be bitwise ORed together without a warning:

```
[Flags]
enum Access
{
  None = 0,
  Read = 1,
  Write = 2,
  Admin = 4
};
// ...
Access userPermissions =
    Access.Read | Access.Write;
```

In addition, this will provide a friendlier implementation of the `ToString()` method for the enumeration. For the above example, `userPermissions.ToString()` will return:

```
Read, Write
```

If the `FlagsAttribute` were not applied, the call would return:

3

6.9 Generics

137. Prefer Generic Types to Non-Typed or Strongly-Typed Classes

.NET 2.0 introduced *generics*, which allow type specialization to occur at runtime. This provides for the definition of type-safe data structures without specifying actual types in the code.

In .NET 1.1, collections are generally implemented either with loose typing (such as the `ArrayList` which contains items of type `Object`), or by creating strongly-typed classes for each concrete type (perhaps using a code generation tool). The former approach compromises type safety and performance; the latter approach requires the creation and maintenance of additional code.

Generics, on the other hand, let you reuse code with any type with full compiler support and type safety.

6.10 Enumerations

138. Use an Enumeration Instead of a Boolean to Improve Readability of Parameters

The meaning of a boolean function parameter is often lost when a developer encounters an invocation of that function. Replacing a boolean parameter with an enumeration can improve the readability of the code and relieves the viewer of the need to review documentation just to discover the meaning of the argument:

```
// What do these parameters mean?
customer.ShowReport(true, true);

// Send the report to both the screen and the
// printer.
```

```
customer.ShowReport(Report.Screen |
                    Report.Printer);
```

139. Use Enumerator Values, Not Integer Constants

Use an enum statement to identify the integral ordinal values that describe a specific concept or property, for example, color, direction, type, mode, etc. Enumerations provide a level of type safety and clarity that simple integer constants cannot.

140. Create a Zero-Valued Enumerator to Indicate an Uninitialized, Invalid, Unspecified, or Default State

Define an enumerator with a name such as "None," "Unspecified," "Unknown," or "Invalid," to provide a type-safe means for testing the validity of an enumeration variable:

```
enum Color
{
  None = 0,
  Red = 1,
  Green = 2,
  Blue = 3
};
```

Make this enumerator the first one in the enumeration. By doing so, you reduce the chance that this enumerator would get overlooked if others add new enumerators to the list, and you also allow the compiler to automatically give the enumerator a value of zero, making it easy to catch an invalid value using a runtime assertion.

141. Validate Enumerated Values

Do not assume that enum values will always be within the defined range, as it is legal to cast an integer value to an enum type, even if that integer does not correspond to a value in the enumeration. For example, given:

```
enum Color
{
  None = 0,
  Red = 1,
  Green = 2,
  Blue = 3
};
```

Though it is unexpected, it is nonetheless legal to write:

```
Color c = (Color) 42;
```

Take appropriate steps to validate the correctness of the enumerated value, particularly if it is constructed from an outside source such as an XML document or a database.

The library function Enum.IsDefined() can be used to determine whether a value exists in an enumeration. However, be aware that Enum.IsDefined() is an expensive runtime function call (using reflection), and that it may not work as expected for combinations of values with the [Flags] attribute.[38] It is preferable to check explicitly for expected values:

```
switch (color)
{
  case Red:
  case Blue:
  case Green:
      ...
      break;
  default:
    throw new ArgumentOutOfRangeException();
      break;
}
```

---

[38] http://blogs.msdn.com/brada/archive/2003/11/29/50903.aspx.

6.11 Type Safety, Casting, and Conversion

142. Avoid Type Casting and Do Not Force Others to Use It

Explicit type casting circumvents the normal type-safety enforcement mechanisms provided by the language. Casting operations may produce subtle errors that may not be detected until somebody else modifies or extends the types and values you are manipulating.

Let the compiler generate type-safe implicit conversions and use casting operators only as a last resort. The most common exceptions to this rule are when referencing objects in object-based collections (though this is not needed when using the generic collections in .NET 2.0) and accessing objects that are referenced through a general event delegate parameter.

When converting objects between types, prefer the type-safe functions in the System.Convert class over direct casts.

143. Prefer the as *Operator to Direct Casts*

A direct cast will throw an InvalidCastException if an object instance is incompatible with a given type. The C# as operator will attempt to cast an object to a specified type and return null if it fails.

If there is a possibility that a cast might fail (for example, you are using an object-based collection that contains a mixture of types), then using the as operator allows you to test for this using a direct conditional statement, rather than handling an exception. See also Rule #144.

144. Use Polymorphism Instead of Frequent is *or* as

The C# is operator will test whether an object instance is compatible with a given type, returning a boolean value. The

C# as operator will attempt to cast an object to a specified type and return null if it fails.

While there are very helpful reasons to use these operators, if your code uses these runtime type checks frequently, you might consider whether a design change is warranted. It may be that judicious use of inheritance and polymorphism can substantially simplify the design.

6.12 Error Handling and Debugging

145. Use Return Codes to Report Expected State Changes

For expected state changes, use a return code, sentinel, or method to report expected state changes. This makes code more readable and the flow of control straightforward. For example, in the course of reading from a file, it is expected that the end of the file will be reached at some point—do not use an exception to report the end-of-file.

146. Use Exceptions to Enforce a Programming Contract

Use *precondition* exceptions if the arguments passed to a method are invalid (for example, ArgumentOutOfRangeException), or if the associated object is in an invalid state when that method is called.

Use *postcondition* exceptions when testing the validity of the results produced by the method or testing that the associated object is in a valid state before method returns.

In general, use an exception if it is relevant to the caller of the method. If the test is indicating a logic error in a method, beyond the caller's control, prefer an assertion (Debug.Assert) instead.

147. Do Not Silently Absorb or Ignore Unexpected Runtime Errors

To create robust software, you need to identify potential sources of runtime errors. If there is any possibility of recovering from the error, you should do so, or at least give your client the opportunity to do so.

Always verify that an operation has completed successfully. If a method returns an indication that it has failed you should determine the cause for the failure and take appropriate action. Check return values and use `try..catch` blocks to detect and respond to errors. Do not create empty `catch` blocks simply to silence an exception (see Rule #152).

If you detect an unrecoverable error, use an assertion or exception to report the error (see Rule #148). If you have access to some form of execution logging facility, log the cause, type, and location of the error prior to taking other action.

148. Use Assertions and Exceptions to Report Unexpected or Unhandled Runtime Errors

You are seldom able to anticipate or recover from all runtime errors. Some errors, such as hardware, third-party software, or internal program logic errors are so severe that no recovery is possible. Program termination may be your only recourse.

You may decide to throw an exception for unexpected runtime errors, but it can be helpful to use `Debug.Assert()` in debug builds of your software: an assertion produces a developer-defined message that can be as descriptive as necessary, and breaks execution directly at the point of failure.

Check all assumptions that your code makes. For example, if an algorithm assumes that a list will only contain a single element in it, assert that. Similarly, use `Debug.Assert()` to check for unexpected states, logic errors, out-of-bounds indices, and so on.

Only use assertions to check for unexpected or unrecoverable errors. If the caller can recover from an error condition, the code should return an error code or throw an exception.

Since the expressions used in assertions are only compiled into debug builds, you should never use "live" code—code that produces side effects—inside these expressions.

149. Use Exceptions to Report Recoverable Errors

Use exceptions to report unexpected but potentially recoverable errors. Some typical examples include the following:

- A file write operation failed because the disk was full.
- A file access operation failed because the disk was removed or unmounted.
- The system could not satisfy a memory-allocation request.
- The system communication software encountered an invalid protocol, sequence, or format.
- A communication request or response was unexpectedly interrupted or canceled by a client.

150. Manage Resources with Try . . . Finally Blocks or Using Statements

In cases where it is critical that your code release an acquired resource (such as a database connection), use a try . . . finally block or a using statement.[39]

---

[39] Note that the "Resource Acquisition is Initialization" (RAII) pattern that is appropriate in many programming languages relies on the construction and destruction of automatically allocated objects to perform resource acquisition and release: in this model, the constructor of an RAII object acquires a resource, and the destructor releases it. However, in the .NET Common Language Runtime, object destruction is managed by the garbage collector, and thus no assumptions can be made about the timing of the release of the resource.

The code in a `finally` block is guaranteed to be executed, regardless of the execution path through the corresponding try block. A referenced object's `Dispose()` method will be invoked at the conclusion of a using block.[40] Both approaches ensure that cleanup code is executed when a block of code is exited, even if that exit occurs as a result of a `throw`.

Consider the following code that uses a database connection:

```
SqlConnection connection =
  new SqlConnection(connectionString);
connection.Open();
...
connection.Dispose();
```

It is important that the database resources be released, even if the control flow is changed by an exception occurring in the unshown code. To ensure this, the `Open()` and `Dispose()` calls can be wrapped in a try ... `finally` block:

```
SqlConnection connection =
  new SqlConnection(connectionString);
try
{
  connection.Open();
  ...
}
finally
{
  connection.Dispose();
}
```

More succinctly, the equivalent logic can be written with a using block:

---

[40] The referenced object must implement the IDisposable interface.

```
using (SqlConnection connection =
        new SqlConnection(connectionString))
{
  connection.Open();
   ...
}
```

Either way, the `Dispose()` method is guaranteed to be called on the `SqlConnection` object, even if an exception is raised within the code block.

151. *Throw the Most Specific Exception Possible*

When throwing an exception, use the most specific exception class that you can; doing so will provide exception handlers with additional information that can aid in handling the exception appropriately. Do not throw exceptions of the base `Exception` class; consider instead more descriptive classes like `NullReferenceException`, `ArgumentOutOfRangeException`, and `FileNotFoundException`, or custom exception classes derived from `ApplicationException`. See also Rules #156 and #157.

152. *Only Catch What You Can Handle*

Only catch an exception if your code is taking concrete action on that exception; otherwise, allow another exception handler the opportunity to catch it. If your handler is only dealing with a specific case (such as when a file is not found), then catch only that specific exception class (such as `FileNotFoundException`), rather than the more general `catch (Exception e)`. See also Rule #156.

153. *Do Not Discard Exception Information If You Throw a New Exception Within a Catch Block*

When you throw a new exception within a `catch()` block, use your exception to augment the information supplied in the original exception. For this purpose, the `Exception` class provides an `InnerException` property and a constructor that accepts an inner `Exception`. If you simply ignore the information provided by the exception you caught, you discard information that might prove valuable at a higher level (see Rule #152).

154. Order Catch Blocks from Most to Least Specific Exception Type

When an exception occurs, the system searches for associated `catch` blocks in the order they appear in the application code, until it finds the first `catch` block that handles the exception. A `catch` block can handle an exception if it specifies the type of the exception or any type derived from it, so beware of code like the following:

```
catch (Exception)
{
  // All exceptions will be caught here ...
}
catch (ApplicationException)
{
  // We'll never get here, because the more general
  // case is matched first.
}
```

155. Don't Throw from Finally

Throwing an exception from a finally block can cause multiple exceptions to be active at one time, and it can be quite difficult to design correctly for this case.[41]

156. Only Create Custom Exceptions If You Think the Caller Will Handle Them Differently

The purpose of custom exception classes is to provide a mechanism for specific exception handlers. If you expect that

---

[41] http://wintellect.com/WEBLOGS/wintellect/archive/2005/03/21/926.aspx.

different categories of exceptions will be handled in very different ways (for example, `ArithmeticException` vs. `IOException`), then provide custom exception classes for each category. However, it is probably overkill to provide a custom class for each specific exception; instead, annotate the exception instance with appropriate diagnostic information.

157. Derive Custom Exceptions from `ApplicationException`, *not* `Exception`

If you are defining a custom exception class, derive from `ApplicationException`, not `Exception`. This convention is used to differentiate application-thrown exceptions from system-thrown exceptions.

158. Use the Built-in Debug Class to Debug Your Code

The `Debug` class provides a number of helpful methods to print diagnostic information and check logic. These calls are only enabled debug builds, so using this class provides a mechanism for making your code more robust without impacting the performance and code size of your release build.

6.13 Events, Delegates, and Threading

159. Use `lock()` *not* `Monitor.Enter()`

The `lock` statement provides convenient shorthand for obtaining a mutual exclusion lock on an object, while ensuring that the lock will be released correctly. A statement of the form:

```
lock(x) ...
```

is equivalent to:

```
System.Threading.Monitor.Enter(x);
try
```

```
{
  ...
}
finally
{
  System.Threading.Monitor.Exit(x);
}
```

See Rule #150.

160. Only Lock on a Private Object

In general, avoid locking on public types or instances beyond the control of your code. It is better to lock on object instances that are private to your class.

7.
Packaging

A "package" may take the form of a single source file, a namespace containing several related classes, or an assembly containing one or more namespaces.

7.1 Files

161. Place Each Namespace-Scope Element in a Separate File

Give each file the same name as the element it contains, using the same case. Doing this has several benefits. Having elements managed with a high level of granularity frequently simplifies packaging decisions. It becomes easier to locate implementations without relying on a tool. File contention for source code checkout, editing, and merging by multiple development team members can be reduced. Note finally that this matches the approach taken by most C++ and Java programmers, which may be an advantage in mixed-language development environments.

162. Use the Element Name as the Filename

In general, put only one public class in each file and give the file the same name as the class (Classname.cs). Modern development environments make it easier to find classes and navigate through files; nonetheless, establishing parallel naming for classes and files generally makes things easier for development teams, particularly larger ones.

7.2 Namespaces

163. Don't Pollute the Framework Namespaces

Don't create types in the System namespaces. It's confusing to users of your code, and can lead to conflicts with the evolving .NET classes.

164. Create a Separate Directory for Each Namespace

Observe a one-to-one mapping between namespaces and directories. This simple organizational structure makes it very easy to find classes and namespaces.

165. Place Types That Are Commonly Used, Changed, and Released Together, or Mutually Dependent on Each Other, into the Same Namespace

This rule encompasses several related package design principles, originally identified by Robert Martin.[42]

The Common Reuse Principle

> A package consists of classes you reuse together. If you use one of the classes in the package, you use all of them.

Place classes and interfaces you usually use together into the same package. Such classes are so closely coupled you cannot use one class without usually using the other. Some examples of closely related types include

- Containers and iterators;
- Database tables, rows, and columns;
- Calendars, dates, and times;
- Points, lines, and polygons.

---

[42] Martin, Robert. "Engineering Notebook: Granularity," C++ Report, Vol. 8, No. 10 (Nov 1996), pp. 57–62.

The Common Closure Principle

A package consists of classes, all closed against the same kind of changes. A change that affects the package affects all the classes in that package.

Combine classes that are likely to change at the same time, for the same reasons, into a single package. If two classes are so closely related that changing one of them usually involves changing the other, then place them in the same package.

The Reuse-Release Equivalence Principle

The unit of reuse is the unit of release. Effective reuse requires tracking of releases from a change control system. The package is the effective unit of reuse and release.

Treating individual classes as a unit of release is not very practical. A typical application may consist of tens or hundreds of classes, so releasing code on a class-by-class basis dramatically complicates the integration and testing process and dramatically increases the overall rate of change within the software.

A package provides a much more convenient mechanism for releasing several classes and interfaces. Each class or interface within a package may undergo several independent revisions between releases, but a package release captures only the latest version of each class and interface. Use packages as the primary unit of release and distribution.

The Acyclic Dependencies Principle

The dependency structure between packages must be a directed acyclic graph; there must be no cycles in the dependency structure.

If two packages directly or indirectly depend on each other, you cannot independently release one without releasing the other because changes in one package often force changes in the other. Such cyclic dependencies dramatically increase the fragility of a system and can eliminate any reduction in schedule realized by assigning the development of each package to separate developers or teams.

Take steps to eliminate cyclic dependencies, either by combining the mutually dependent packages or by introducing a new package of abstractions that both packages can depend on instead of each other.

166. Isolate Unstable Classes in Separate Assemblies

Avoid placing unstable classes in the same package with stable classes. If you use packages as your principal unit of release and distribution, users can gain access to the latest changes in the unstable classes only if you re-release the entire package. Each time you release the package, your users must absorb the cost of reintegrating and retesting against all the classes in the package, although many may not have changed.

Separate unstable classes from stable classes to reduce the code footprint affected by new releases of code, thereby reducing the impact on users of that code.

167. Maximize Abstraction to Maximize Stability

This rule derives from the following design principle.[43]

The Stable Abstractions Principle

> The stability exhibited by a package is directly proportional to its level of abstraction. The more abstract a

---

[43] Ibid.

package is, the more stable it tends to be. The more concrete a package is, the more unstable it tends to be.

Use stable abstractions to create stable packages. Capture high-level, stable concepts in abstract classes and interfaces and provide implementations using concrete classes. Separate abstract classes and interfaces from the concrete classes to form stable and unstable packages. This ensures that the derived classes in the unstable packages depend on the abstract superclasses and interfaces in the stable packages.

168. Capture High-Level Design and Architecture as Stable Abstractions Organized into Stable Namespace

To plan and manage a software development effort successfully, the top-level design must stabilize quickly and remain that way. No development manager can hope to accurately plan, estimate, schedule, and allocate resources if the architecture of the system continues to change.

Once the design of the high-level architecture is complete, use packages to separate the stable parts of the design from the volatile implementation. Create packages to capture the high-level abstractions of the design. Place the detailed implementation of those abstractions into separate packages that depend on the high-level abstract packages.

7.3 Assemblies

169. Match Assembly and Namespace Names

Using the same name should ensure that your assembly is uniquely named. The contents of an assembly are also transparent to users when adding references.

170. Avoid Making Difficult-to-Change Assemblies Dependent on Assemblies That Are Easy to Change

This rule derives from the following design principle.[44]

The Stable Dependencies Principle

> The dependencies between packages should be oriented in the direction of increasing stability. A package should only depend on packages more stable than it is.

If a package containing difficult-to-change types is dependent on a package that contains easy, or likely to change, types, then the dependent package effectively acts to impede change in the volatile package.

In a software system, especially one that is incrementally developed, some packages always remain somewhat volatile. The developers of such a system must feel free to modify and extend these volatile packages to complete the implementation of the system and must be able to do so without worrying too much about downstream effects.

Do not create a package that depends on less-stable packages. If necessary, create new abstractions that can be used to invert the relationship between the stable code and the unstable code.

171. Increment Assembly Versions Manually

Assembly versions are used by the .NET runtime to determine whether two types match. Increment the `AssemblyVersion-Attribute` manually, rather than relying on the default versioning scheme. This allows you to enforce your organization's

---

[44] Martin, Robert. "Engineering Notebook: Stability," C++ Report, Vol. 9, No. 2 (Feb 1997).

build policies, such as specifying whether a release is a major, minor, maintenance, or engineering revision.

172. Expose Individual Classes to COM, Not Entire Assemblies

Only expose what is necessary. Set the `ComVisible` attribute to false at the assembly level, and enable for individual classes.

```
[ComVisible(true)]
class MyClass
{
  ...
}
```

173. Place Classes with Unsafe Code into Separate Assemblies

Some environments prohibit the use of unsafe code. If you isolate unsafe code into separate assemblies, then you can still use the other assemblies.

174. Statically Link Native Code

Sometimes you need to use native code. One option is to reference native dynamic libraries (DLLs) using the `DllImport` attribute. This means that the referenced DLL must accompany your .NET assemblies during deployment. However, DLLs cannot be placed in the global assembly cache, and must be in a directory in the user's path.

In some cases, the better solution is to create a Managed C++ assembly that links in a native static library (LIB). The resulting assembly can be deployed in the same manner as other .NET assemblies.

Summary

1. General Principles

1. *Adhere to the style of the original*
2. *Adhere to the Principle of Least Astonishment*
3. *Do it right the first time*
4. *Document any deviations*
5. *Consider using a code-checking tool to enforce coding standards*

2. Formatting

6. *Include white space*
7. *Use indented block statements*
8. *Indent statements after a label*
9. *Do not use "hard" tabs*
10. *Break long statements into multiple lines*
11. *Choose one style for brace placement*
12. *Always use block statements in control flow constructs*
13. *Group using directives at the top of a source file*
14. *Organize source code into regions*
15. *Order class elements by access*
16. *Declare each variable and attribute separately*

3. Naming

17. *Use meaningful names*
18. *Name according to meaning not type*
19. *Use familiar names*
20. *Do not use case to differentiate names*
21. *Avoid excessively long names*
22. *Join the vowel generation—use complete words*
23. *Avoid abbreviations unless the full name is excessive*
24. *Format abbreviations like regular words*
25. *Use uppercase and underscores for preprocessor symbols*
26. *Add a unique prefix to preprocessor names*
27. *Use Pascal case for namespaces, classes, structures, properties, enumerations, constants, and functions*
28. *Use nouns to name compound types*
29. *Pluralize the names of collections*
30. *Suffix abstract base types with "Base"*
31. *Append the pattern name to classes implementing a design pattern*
32. *Use a single capital letter for generic parameters*
33. *Use singular names for enumerations*
34. *Use plural names for bitfields*
35. *Prefix interface names with a capital letter "I"*
36. *Use nouns or adjectives when naming interfaces*
37. *Name properties after the item they get or set*
38. *Avoid redundant property names*
39. *Name boolean properties to indicate their boolean nature*
40. *Use Pascal case for method names*

41. *Use verbs to name methods*
42. *Avoid redundant method names*
43. *Use camel case for variable and method parameter names*
44. *Use nouns to name variables*
45. *Add a prefix or suffix to member variable names to distinguish them from other variables*
46. *Give constructor and property parameters the same name as the fields to which they are assigned*
47. *Use a set of standard names for "throwaway" variables and parameters*
48. *Suffix custom attribute implementations with "Attribute"*
49. *Use an organization name for the root namespace, and narrow by project, product, or group*
50. *Clearly distinguish the event-handling parts through appropriate names*
51. *Suffix custom exception types with* `Exception`

4. Documentation

52. *Document your software interface for those who must use it*
53. *Document your implementation for those who must maintain it*
54. *Keep your comments and code synchronized*
55. *Document software elements as early as possible*
56. *Write for an international audience*
57. *Add copyright, license, and author information to the top of every file*

58. *Make liberal use of the documentation mechanism built into the C# language*

59. *Document important preconditions, postconditions, and invariant conditions*

60. *Document thread synchronization requirements*

61. *Document known defects and deficiencies*

62. *Use the active voice to describe actors and passive voice to describe actions*

63. *Use "this" rather than "the" when referring to instances of the current class*

64. *Add internal comments only if they will aid others in understanding your code*

65. *Explain why the code does what it does*

66. *Avoid C-style block comments*

67. *Use one-line comments to explain implementation details*

68. *Avoid the use of end-line comments*

69. *Label closing braces in highly nested control structure*

70. *Use keywords to mark pending work, unresolved issues, defects, and bug fixes*

71. *Label empty statements*

5. Design

72. *Do not be afraid to do engineering*

73. *Choose simplicity over elegance*

74. *Recognize the cost of reuse*

75. *Program by contract*

76. *Choose an appropriate engineering methodology*

6. Programming

100. *Use partial types only to support machine-generated code*

101. *Do not rely on operator precedence in complex expressions*

102. *Do not test for equality with* `true` *or* `false`

103. *Replace repeated, non-trivial expressions with equivalent methods*

104. *Avoid complex statements in ternary conditions.*

105. *Use* `Object.Equals()` *to test for object identity of reference types*

106. *Avoid* `break` *and* `continue` *in iteration statements*

107. *Avoid multiple* `return` *statements in methods*

108. *Do not use* `goto`

109. *Do not use* `try ... throw ... catch` *to manage control flow*

110. *Declare for-loop iteration variables inside of* `for` *statements*

111. *Add a default case label to the end of all switch statements*

112. *Define small classes and small methods*

113. *Build fundamental classes from standard types*

114. *Avoid the use of virtual base classes in user-extensible class hierarchies*

115. *Declare the access level of all members*

116. *Mark classes sealed to prevent unwanted derivation*

117. *Avoid the use of* `internal` *declarations*

118. *Avoid the use of* `new` *to hide members of a derived type*

119. *Limit the use of* `base` *to subclass constructors and overridden methods*

120. *Override* operator== *and* operator!= *when overriding the* Equals() *method*

121. *Consider overriding the implicit string conversion operator when overriding the* ToString() *method*

122. *Implement a method in terms of its opposite*

123. *Initialize all variables*

124. *Always construct objects in a valid state*

125. *Declare an explicit default constructor for added clarity and COM interoperability*

126. *Make constructors protected to prohibit direct instantiation*

127. *Always list any base constructors in the initializer list of a derived constructor*

128. *Use nested constructors to eliminate redundant code*

129. *Implement* IDisposable *on classes referencing external resources*

130. *Declare all fields with private access, and use properties to provide access*

131. *Use properties only for simple, inexpensive, order-independent access*

132. *Avoid passing an excessive number of parameters*

133. *Validate parameter values*

134. *Deprecate APIs using* System.ObsoleteAttribute

135. *Consider whether new classes should be serializable*

136. *Use the* System.FlagsAttribute *to designate bitfields*

137. *Prefer generic types to non-typed or strongly-typed classes*

138. *Use an enumeration instead of a boolean to improve readability of parameters*

139. *Use enumerator values, not integer constants*

140. *Create a zero-valued enumerator to indicate an uninitialized, invalid, unspecified, or default state*

141. *Validate enumerated values*

142. *Avoid type casting and do not force others to use it*

143. *Prefer the* as *operator to direct casts*

144. *Use polymorphism instead of frequent* is *or* as

145. *Use return codes to report expected state changes*

146. *Use exceptions to enforce a programming contract*

147. *Do not silently absorb or ignore unexpected runtime errors*

148. *Use assertions and exceptions to report unexpected or unhandled runtime errors*

149. *Use exceptions to report recoverable errors*

150. *Manage resources with try . . . finally blocks or using statements*

151. *Throw the most specific exception possible*

152. *Only catch what you can handle*

153. *Do not discard exception information if you throw a new exception within a catch block*

154. *Order catch blocks from most to least specific exception type*

155. *Don't throw from finally*

156. *Only create custom exceptions if you think the caller will handle them differently*

157. *Derive custom exceptions from* ApplicationException, *not* Exception

158. *Use the built-in Debug class to debug your code*

159. *Use* lock() *not* Monitor.Enter()

160. *Only lock on a private object*

7. Packaging

Glossary

abstract class
A class that exists only as a superclass of another class and can never be directly instantiated.

abstract data type
Defines a type that may have many implementations. Abstract data types encapsulate data with operations on that data such that the user of the type need not be concerned with the implementation. Abstract data types include things like dates, strings, stacks, queues, and trees.

abstract method
A method that has no implementation. Also known as a "pure virtual" method; this method must be overridden in derived classes to be used.

abstract type
Defines the type for a set of objects, where each object must also belong to a set of objects that conform to a known subtype of the abstract type. An abstract type may have one or more implementations.

abstraction
The process and result of extracting the common or general characteristics from a set of similar entities.

accessor
A method that gets the value of an object member variable.

active object
An object that possesses its own thread of control.

acyclic dependency

A dependency relationship where one entity has a direct or indirect dependency on a second entity, but the second entity has no direct or indirect dependency on the first.

aggregation

An association representing a whole–part containment relationship.

architecture

A description of the organization and structure of a software system.

argument

Data item bound to a parameter in a method call.

assembly

A group of .NET files versioned and deployed as a unit.

assertion

A statement about the truth of a logical expression.

attribute

Annotations to programming elements such as types, fields, methods, and properties that control application behavior at run time.

behavior

The activities and effects produced by an object in response to an event or method call.

binary compatible

A situation where one version of a software component may be directly and transparently substituted for another version of that component without recompiling the component's clients.

block statement

The language construct that combines one or more statement expressions into a single compound statement, by enclosing them in curly braces: "{...}".

boxing

The conversion of a **value type** instance to an object, by making a copy and embedding it in a new object.

camel case

Use of lowercase for the first word, and upper case for each subsequent word that appears in an identifier. This provide a visual cue for separating the individual words within each name. Also known as "lower camel case." See Rule #43.

class

The formal definition of an object. The class acts as the template from which an instance of an object is created at run time. The class defines the properties of the object and the methods used to control the object's behavior.

class hierarchy

A set of classes associated by inheritance relationships.

client

An entity that requests a service from another entity.

CLR

See **Common Language Runtime (CLR)**.

CLS

See **Common Language Specification (CLS)**.

cohesion

The degree to which two or more entities belong together or relate to each other.

COM

Component Object Model: a previous specification by Microsoft for writing reusable software components.

Common Language Runtime (CLR)

The engine that executes **managed code**.

Common Language Specification (CLS)

A specification of language features supported by the **Common Language Runtime**.

component

A physical and discrete software entity that conforms to a set of interfaces.

composition

A form of aggregation where an object is composed of other objects.

concrete class

A completely specified class that may be directly instantiated. A concrete class defines a specific implementation for an abstract class or type.

concrete type

A type that may be directly instantiated. A concrete type may refine or extend an abstract type.

concurrency

The degree by which two or more activities (threads of execution) occur or make progress at the same time.

constraint

A restriction on the value or behavior of an entity.

constructor

A special method that initializes a new instance of a class.

container

An object whose purpose is to contain and manipulate other objects.

contract

A clear description of the responsibilities and constraints that apply between a client and a type, class, or method.

coupling

The degree to which two or more entities are dependent on each other.

critical section

A block of code that allows only one thread at a time to enter and execute the instructions within that block. Any threads attempting to enter a critical section while another thread is already executing within that section are blocked until the original thread exits.

cyclic dependency

A dependency relationship where one entity has a direct or indirect dependency on a second entity and the second entity also has a direct or indirect dependency on the first.

data type

A primitive or built-in type that represents pure data and has no distinct identity as an object.

delegate

A reference type used to encapsulate a method with a specific signature; roughly corresponds to a C++ function pointer.

delegation

The act of passing a message, and responsibility, from one object to a second object to elicit a desired response.

dependency

A relationship where the semantic characteristics of one entity rely upon and constrain the semantic characteristics of another entity.

derivation

The process of defining a new type or class by specializing or extending the behavior and attributes of an existing type or class.

domain

An area of expertise, knowledge, or activity.

encapsulation

The degree to which an appropriate mechanism hides the internal data, structure, and implementation of an object or other entity.

enumeration

A type that defines a list of named values that make up the allowable range for values of that type.

factor

The act of reorganizing one or more types or classes by extracting responsibilities from existing classes and synthesizing new classes to handle these responsibilities.

field

An instance variable or data member of an object.

fundamental data type

A type that typically requires only one implementation and is commonly used to construct other, more useful, types. Dates, complex numbers, linked lists, and vectors are examples of common fundamental data types.

garbage collection

A process in which dynamically allocated blocks of memory are reclaimed while a program executes.

generalization

The process of extracting the common or general characteristics from a set of similar entities to create a new entity that possesses these common characteristics.

global assembly cache (GAC)

A cache that stores .NET assemblies shared by many applications on a computer.

implementation

The concrete realization of a contract defined by a type, abstract class, or interface. The actual code.

implementation class

A concrete class that provides an implementation for a type, abstract class, or interface.

implementation inheritance

The action or mechanism by which a subclass inherits the implementation and interface from one or more super-classes.

inheritance

The mechanism by which more specialized entities acquire or incorporate the responsibilities or implementation of more generalized entities.

instance

The result of instantiating a class—the concrete representation of an object.

instantiation

The action or mechanism by which a type or class is reified to create an actual object. The act of allocating and initializing an object from a class.

interface

The methods exposed by a type, class, or object. Also a set of operations that define an abstract service.

internal access

An access modifier for types and members; members marked with the `internal` keyword appear as `public` to classes in the same assembly, but `private` to classes outside the assembly.

invariant

An expression that describes the well-defined, legal states of an object.

JavaDoc

A tool that generates API documentation in HTML format from Java source code.

keyword

A language construct. Keywords are reserved and cannot be used as identifiers.

lazy evaluation

When an implementation delays the evaluation of an expression until the last possible moment. With respect to object lifetimes, this can mean delaying object construction and initialization until the object is actually required. The intent is to gain efficiency by avoiding unnecessary work.

local variable

A variable that is automatically allocated and initialized on the call "stack." Includes parameter variables that are bound to function arguments.

lower camel case

See **camel case**.

managed code

Code that is executed by the **common language runtime** environment rather than directly by the operating system.

method

The implementation of an operation. An operation defined by an interface or class.

MSDN

Microsoft Developer Network. A group of services that provide technical information to software developers using Microsoft technologies.

multiple inheritance

Inheritance relationship where a class inherits from two or more superclasses.

mutator

A method that sets the value of an object member variable.

mutex

A synchronization mechanism used to provide mutually exclusive access to a resource. A mutex is generally used to serialize access to a critical section.

See **critical section**.

namespace

A logical naming scheme for grouping related items.

native code

Code that has been compiled to processor-specific machine code.

native type

See **built-in type**.

nested class

A class defined within the scope of another class.

object

The result of instantiating a class. An entity with state, behavior, and identity.

operation

A service that may be requested from an object to effect behavior. Alternatively viewed as a message sent from a client to an object.

package

A mechanism organizing and naming a collection of related classes.

parameter

A variable that is bound to an argument value passed into a method.

Pascal case

Capitalization of the first letter of each word to provide a visual cue for separating the individual words within a name, for example, "BackgroundColor." Also known as "upper camel case." See Rules #27, #40.

polymorphic
A method that can operate correctly on a variety of types. Also, a trait or characteristic of an object whereby that object can appear as several different types at the same time.

polymorphism
The concept or mechanism by which objects of different types inherit the responsibility for implementing the same operation, but respond differently to the invocation of that operation.

postcondition
A constraint or assertion that must hold true following the completion of an operation.

precondition
A constraint or assertion that must hold true at the start of an operation.

primitive type
See **built-in type**.

private access
An access-control characteristic applied to class inheritance relationships and class members. Class members declared with the `private` access modifier are only accessible to code in the same class and are not inherited by subclasses.

property
A class member that is like a public field, which special syntax for get and set accessor methods.

protected access
An access-control characteristic applied to class inheritance relationships and class members. Class members declared with the `protected` access modifier are accessible to code in the same class and are inherited by subclasses.

public access
An access-control characteristic applied to class inheritance relationships and class members. Class members declared

with the `public` access modifier are accessible anywhere the class is accessible and are inherited by subclasses.

qualifier
A name or value used to locate or identify a particular entity within a set of similar entities.

realization
A relationship where one entity abides by or the contract specified by another entity.

reference type
A data type that is represented by a reference to the type's actual value. See also **value type**.

responsibility
A purpose or obligation assigned to a type.

role
The set of responsibilities associated with an entity that participates in a specific relationship.

serialization
The process of granting a single thread access to a critical section while blocking all other threads; in this context, serialization is usually synonymous with synchronization. See **synchronization** and **critical section**. Serialization also refers to the encoding of a data structure into a sequence of bytes.

service
One or more operations provided by a type, class, or object to accomplish useful work on behalf of one or more clients.

signature
An interface specification for a method. It includes the method's class, type of return value and the types of its formal parameters.

state
The condition or value of an object.

static type checking

Compile-time verification of the assumptions made about the use of object reference and data value types.

subclass

A class that inherits attributes and methods from another class. Also known as a "derived class" or a "child class."

subtype

The more specific type in a specialization–generalization relationship.

superclass

A class from which a subclass inherits attributes and methods. Also known as a "base class" or "parent class."

supertype

The more general type in a specialization–generalization relationship.

synchronization

The process or mechanism used to preserve the invariant states of a program or object in the presence of multiple threads.

See **serialization** and **critical section**.

thread

A single flow of control within a process that executes a sequence of instructions in an independent execution context.

type

Defines the common responsibilities, behavior, and operations associated with a set of similar objects. A type does not define an implementation.

unboxing

The conversion of an object instance to a **value type**. See also **boxing**.

unmanaged code
> Code that is executed directly by the operating system, outside the **common language runtime** environment. See also **managed code**.

upper camel case
> See **Pascal case**.

value type
> A data type that is represented by the type's actual value. See also **boxing, reference type, unboxing**.

variable
> A typed, named container for holding object references or data values.

visibility
> The degree to which an entity may be accessed from outside of a particular scope.

Bibliography

Abrams, Brad. *.NET Framework Standard Library Annotated Reference, Volume 1: Base Class Library and Extended Numerics Library.* (Reading, Massachusetts: Addison-Wesley, 2004).

Abrams, Brad, and Krzysztof Cwalina. "The Art of Building a Reusable Class Library." Pre-conference presentation, Microsoft Professional Developers Conference 2005. http://www.microsoft.com/downloads/details.aspx?FamilyID=ea01d6ed-ad11-4103-be2b-defc559e3d97&displaylang=en

Box, Don. *Essential .NET, Volume I: The Common Language Runtime.* (Reading, Massachusetts: Addison-Wesley, 2002).

Brackett, George. "Class 6: Designing for Communication: Layout, Structure, Navigation for Nets and Webs." In "Course T525: Designing Educational Experiences for Networks and Webs." (Harvard Graduate School of Education, 26 Aug 1999).

Cargill, Tom. "C++ Gotchas: Tutorial Notes." p. 13. Distributed at these seminars: http://www.profcon.com/profcon/Gotchas.htm

Cwalina, Krzysztof, and Brad Abrams. *Framework Design Guidelines: Conventions, Idioms, and Patterns for Reusable .NET Libraries.* (Reading, Massachusetts: Addison-Wesley, 2005).

Dijkstra, Edsger W. "Go To Statement Considered Harmful," Communications of the ACM, Vol. 11, No. 3 (Mar 1968), pp. 147–148.

Gamma, Eric et al. *Design Patterns: Elements of Reusable Object-Oriented Software.* (Reading, Massachusetts: Addison-Wesley, 1995), pp. 325–330.

Hejlsberg, Anders, Scott Wiltamuth, and Peter Golde. *The C# Programming Language*. (Reading, Massachusetts: Addison-Wesley, 2003).

Karabatsos, Jim. "When does this document apply?" In "Visual Basic Programming Standards." (GUI Computing Ltd., 22 Mar 1996).

Kernighan, Brian, and P. J. Plauger. *The Elements of Programming Style*. (New York: McGraw-Hill, 1988), p. 118.

Lea, Doug. *Concurrent Programming in Java*™: *Design Principles and Patterns*. (Reading, Massachusetts: Addison-Wesley, 1997), pp. 1–2.

Liskov, Barbara, and Guttag, John. *Abstraction and Specification in Program Development*. (New York: McGraw-Hill, 1986).

Martin, Robert. "Engineering Notebook: The Open-Closed Principle," C++ Report, Vol. 8, No. 1 (Jan 1996).

Martin, Robert. "Engineering Notebook," C++ Report, Vol. 8, No. 3 (Mar 1996).

Martin, Robert. "Engineering Notebook: Granularity," C++ Report, Vol. 8, No. 10 (Nov 1996), pp. 57–62.

Martin, Robert. "Engineering Notebook: Stability," C++ Report, Vol. 9, No. 2 (Feb 1997).

McConnell, Steve. *Code Complete*. (Redmond, Washington: Microsoft Press, 1993), pp. 337–338.

Meyer, Bertrand. *Object-Oriented Software Construction*. (Englewood Cliffs, New Jersey: Prentice Hall, 2000).

Prosise, Jeff. *Programming Microsoft .NET*. (Redmond, Washington: Microsoft Press, 2002).

Richter, Jeffrey. *Applied Microsoft .NET Framework Programming*. (Redmond, Washington: Microsoft Press, 2002).

Schmidt, Douglas C., and Harrison, Tim. *Pattern Languages of Program Design*. (Reading, Massachusetts: Addison-Wesley, 1997).

Index